Unexpected Grace

A Discovery of Healing
Through Surrender

By June Hyjek

For information about this title or to order other books and/or electronic
media, contact the publisher:

 Publishing Directions, LLC
50 Lovely St.
PO Box 715
Avon, CT 06001

Library of Congress Control Number: 2013931526

ISBN: 978-1-928782-43-8
Printed in the United States of America
Cover and Interior design by 1106 Design, Phoenix, AZ

"Two roads diverged in a wood, and I —
I took the one less traveled by,
And that has made all the difference."
Robert Frost
"The Road Not Taken"

These pages are dedicated to my
loving and supportive husband, Peter.
Each moment I spend with you is a source
of joy, inspiration and love. Each time you
hold me in your arms, I know that is where
I truly belong. I will love you always.
Thank you for walking by my side, even
as I choose the road less traveled.
With all my love,
June

Acknowledgments

There are many people without whom this book would not have existed, and I owe them my eternal gratitude for sharing my journey with me and helping me to tell my story.

Through these pages, you will hear a little about my husband, Peter, who supports me unconditionally and is the real driver behind converting this project from a dream to a reality. He "made me" publish this and I cannot thank him enough!

You will also hear about my physical therapist, Brian Swanson. It would be safe to say that without his constant encouragement, gentle (and sometimes not-so-gentle) pushing, as well as his belief in me and quiet wisdom, I would not have had the strength to go through all this and have a story to tell at all. I thank him for standing by my side all these years with patience and compassion.

My gratitude also goes to Brian Jud, President of Publishing Directions, LLC . . . my publisher, my friend, and the first one to read my manuscript. He believed in this long before I did. Thank you for making this possible.

In these pages, you'll also hear the words of my beloved teachers, Dory Dzinski and Richard Gould. I thank them for their presence in my life, always there with arms open—ready to catch me should I fall, prop me up when I get tired, or simply hold me in my fear.

My gratitude also goes out to those dear friends who walked with me on this path and responded to my emails with their own loving words of support and guidance. Namaste. I bow to you.

And of course, thank you to the incredible people at 1106 Design, who were behind the creation of the book itself. In particular, I'd like to thank Ronda Rawlins, my project manager and the gentle shepherd through the whole process. You guided me through difficult decisions with compassion and enthusiasm. Your unending patience would rival that of Buddha! My sincere thanks go to all of you at 1106 for the way you lovingly cared for my words and turned them into something beautiful to share. Thank you for giving me "Unexpected Grace."

Table of Contents

Foreword

Life is so fascinating, isn't it? As we watch the matrix levels reveal themselves and see the tapestries being woven, hindsight allows us to open our eyes wide and say, "Wow!" at the staggering precision of universal timing.

A tiny example in my own life was that a week or so before June even called to ask me to write this Foreword, Manchester Community College put me into the Lowe building for one of my classes, which is not where I am typically located. But hey, okay, no problem. As I walked to my classroom, I passed a corner in the student lounge that brought back a sweet memory. After one of my classes in the same building many years ago, I was walking out with a group of the students, and one of them spotted a piano. She casually strolled over, sat down, and suddenly the student center was filled with a strong and beautiful melody.

This is one of my favorite memories of June — sitting down at a piano in the Lowe building of MCC, playing like a concert pianist! Her talents unfold like the proverbial layers of an onion.

I find metaphors and symbology fascinating. Take her name — June — the month in the center of the year. And the letter J — positioned as one of the center letters of the alphabet. Some of our greatest and strongest master teachers and influences toward balance, strength, and finding and living from your center, have names beginning with J such as Jesus and Jupiter, Janus and Juno (particularly interesting as gods often associated with war) . . . And lo and behold, the letter itself looks like a hook. This is not only representative of the literal metal hooks in June's back, as a result of numerous back surgeries, but also representative of the hooks that we as humans get connected to in our thinking, patterns, habits, etc. June, through her challenges, was able to identify some of her major hooks and work toward getting herself "off the hook"!

This book is possibly the longest thank you note ever! Guinness, where are you?! For those of us who were recipients of June's emails, she settled into the very fiber of our beings. She was with us every day. I found myself thinking about her, praying for her, wondering how she was doing. Because we are June and she is us. She has put into words our own silent fears, questions, and disappointments. And with her, we have shouted our joys! At many points along the way, June must have heard, time and time again, "You know, June? This would make a great book!" So now, I am sitting here in the front row applauding her for this creation. You know those books that you sink into and when they're done, you just sit there with the book (or Nook or Kindle) in your hands, just digesting the contents and energy of the book . . . and wanting a bit more? This is one of those books.

I love the way she has set up this book. There are two Junes speaking in this story — the June that created the journal and email entries long ago, and the June that is reading them now and responding as who she is today, with only the great insight and understanding that hindsight is able to provide. I find myself smiling and laughing out loud as I read. It is very easy to bond with June and I think you, the reader, will develop concern about her right away. And I even wonder if stand-up comedy is in her future! Again, another layer of the talent onion!

Sweet, strong June. She is like a woman-child that you want to hug and comfort. Warrior-like, ever pushing forward, but when you look into her eyes, you can readily see that little girl reaching out to be loved, so tired from pushing so hard, needing to prove herself. When little did she know at the time, but she was fully and completely loved just because she existed. Just because she was . . . simply . . . June. You will see yourself in June — striving, battling, more and more. And I feel as if her words will encourage you to put down your sword and shield, as well, and just be with what is.

As she relays her remarkable journey, June helps reinforce for us that we are not our bodies; we are not our accomplishments; we are not the "hats" that we wear. We are worthy of love, respect, and caring simply because we exist. Our deservability can be quite uncomfortable when we first put it on. It just doesn't seem to fit right because so many of us have been groomed to believe that we must prove our worth. We are familiar with phrases such as "No pain, no gain." "It's not worth having if you don't have to work for it." Such fallacies! It is delightful to read along as June reaches the point of discovery that we are all royalty — we are all deserving — we are all special! As I have always told my own students, by special, I do not mean *better than*, but unique, each with our own endearing and frustrating qualities. Each perfectly imperfect! Through her story, June helps to emphasize that each one of us is a prince and princess, deserving of respect, tenderness, compassion, caring, and anything else that we need to live from a healthy perspective. I would recommend meditating on your personal image of your prince- or princess-self. What does your throne look like? What are you wearing? Do you have a crown or scepter? This does not have any connection at all with control over others, your better-ness, or anything else having to do with ego. Just the simple and elegant expression of your divine self, your brilliance, your beauty, your soul . . .

I owned a small healing practice from 1999 through 2006 called Ways of Gentle Strength. My logo image was a stalk of wheat that I drew myself and turned into a stamp that I used to create my brochures. My theme was that we need to live like the wheat, gracefully bending when winds of challenge come, but standing up straight and tall when the challenge has passed. As we turn the pages of this book, we see June constantly bending and straightening, the epitome of this image. So beautiful . . .

You, dear reader, will learn that June suffers from severe back issues. In looking at the psychospiritual correlation of back pain and lack of feeling supported, this process has indeed shown June that, beyond a shadow of a doubt, she IS supported. She does not have to keep holding up the uber-heavy sword and shield she talks about carrying throughout her life. In fact, swords actually look very nice as wall decorations. The real courage and bravery comes in the revelation of the soul — in its simple complexity — and in the realization of that well-worn truthful expression — We Are All One.

At one point, June noticed that without the brace, she was able to stand up straight more easily. Funny, that. Giving up the warrior piece, something you'll see June struggle with throughout this process, and yet being able to support yourself more easily. As the reader, we are able to watch June flip flop, in and out of warrior, when she least expects it. We read some words and say, Ooops, it's up again! And lo and behold, in the very next email, she's caught it and has rebalanced. And then we see it again. June educates us that life causes us to twist and turn, deny and accept, over and over. And that's OK. We're OK. As June reminds us many times, it's all in how we handle what is. In the Worcester Armory up in Massachusetts, there is a glorious collection of suits of armor. I wonder if June's suit is up there?

It's interesting to watch June's efforts to bend in attempts to make herself into a non-Type A person, but then witness the amazing revelation come to pass. She IS a Type A person, and therein lies the graceful acceptance of no longer judging her Type A-ness, but embracing it, loving it, and bringing it out into her personality when it is needed at the right time and place. And being so engrained as that pattern is, the Type A-ness will spring into action and get whatever is needed done with ease, accuracy, and confidence. Sure sounds like a keeper to me. And then it can go dormant and the princess can rest again. What a beautiful balance . . .

When you have finished reading June's story, and are holding her words in your hands, you may consider reading this Foreword once again. Some of the ideas presented here may hold deeper meaning and connection for you in your own life and healing process.

So, as June has set the example for us with regard to celebrating each precious moment of our lives, let's all go into our refrigerators and pull out that expensive champagne, no longer waiting for some momentous occasion to warrant enjoying it, an occasion that may never come or be so far in the future that all of the champagne bubbles would have long since popped. Open it up, toast, and drink it now! Today! For to be present today, living, breathing, loving, is most certainly a wonderfully sacred and precious thing to celebrate! Enjoy what is . . . for how quickly we know it becomes something else. Better? Worse? No . . . just different. We never walk alone . . . let's all carry a piece of June inside of us, continuing to teach us balance, grace, self-awareness, and new ways to get ourselves off the hook!!!

Namaste,

Dory Dzinski, LPC

Dory Dzinski is a Licensed Professional Counselor in private practice in the historic Collinsville section of Canton, CT. Since the mid-80's, Dory has had an avid interest in spirituality and has been teaching spiritually based classes since 1998. She is a Professional Life Coach, the editor/publisher of Connecticut's leading magazine on spirituality and holistic health, The Door Opener, and is past president of the Connecticut Holistic Health Association. She continues to teach many classes in spiritually related topics and thoroughly enjoys assisting her clients along their spiritual paths.

SECTION ONE

Help! My Center Is Crooked!

Prologue

L ife is what happens when you're busy making other plans.

I think it was John Lennon who said that in one of his songs. I unfortunately discovered that it couldn't be more true. One day, when I really wasn't looking and everything seemed normal — my life changed. Completely, irrevocably, unexpectedly, instantly. I thought I had everything in order and well planned out, but no, I was apparently mistaken. And I wasn't really happy about it. I found myself facing the biggest challenge of my life and dealing with more pain than I ever thought possible, both physically and emotionally.

I guess life has a way of eventually forcing you to deal with your crap. It may start with a nudge, but if you don't listen or pay attention to the lessons, that nudge can become a really big slap. Well, you could say I got whacked. And I had much to learn.

A year later now, I'm beginning to feel as though I'm getting through it all pretty well. And although some of the lessons I learned weren't the ones I expected, I realized I had a story to tell. That slap still stings, but unless you're Buddha, growth is usually a process, not an overnight epiphany.

I'm not a doctor, or a therapist, or a medical person at all. So I can't give you any answers on how to magically overcome pain or illness, or tell you that my way is the best. But having struggled with pain and a debilitating condition for more than half my life, I figure I've learned a thing or two to share.

I have scoliosis. It's a condition more than six million people in the US struggle with, mostly women. Scoliosis is characterized by a curvature of the spine, which leaves you with a serious deformity in a society that praises beauty. But that's just its most prominent symptom. The spine is your physical center (and metaphorically your emotional center as well). So a condition that twists your spine in horrible ways has to affect other major bodily systems — muscular, hormonal, digestive, neurological . . . and it's degenerative. In short, you end up feeling like a walking medical nightmare, and a deformed one at that. And the really bad part? Not only do doctors not know how to cure it, they don't even know what causes it.

Scoliosis doesn't get much attention these days. There are lots of other diseases that kill people and we absolutely need to put much of our resources there. And although people have died from the complications that come from scoliosis, the disease itself doesn't actually kill anyone.

But I would be less than honest if I didn't admit the physical and emotional pain that has come from having scoliosis has often left me wishing it did.

I've tried so many treatment options — from both the Western and Eastern sides of medicine. Surgery (six total), physical therapy, muscle relaxers, pain medicines, Chi Kung, Pilates, nutrition, meditation, past-life regression, Reiki, massage, reflexology. Some things worked some of the time and some worked better than others. And a few of these practices have become an integral part of how I live my life. After my last round of surgeries (the ones that really changed my life), I discovered that each of these modalities and treatments is only part of the answer. Somehow, the real solution rested in me, deep inside, in my core. The part that was missing to truly manage my condition was me. While I walked around with a painful, crooked spine (my physical center), I began to realize my emotional or spiritual center had to be off as well. In fact, many therapists now believe physical disease can be a manifestation of an emotional issue. If I was going to stop this Merry-Go-Round ride of one surgery after another, I would have to approach my recovery this time a little differently. Was there something about how I was living that was creating this crooked spine?

And so I started my journey, entering a new phase in my life, by saying this to myself out loud: "Help! My center is crooked!"

In that one statement, I made it clear to myself that it was more than my spine that was the problem. I would need the help of others to get through it. I didn't know where that would lead me, and I struggled to surrender to the process without trying to change or manage anything — something really hard for a recovering Type-A personality to do. I tried to let myself be exactly where I was and just listen to what my body was telling me.

My story is not the triumph of overcoming pain. It's the ongoing journey of learning to be exactly where I am now, good or bad, accepting that place and living in it. I know that sounds like mumbo-jumbo, holistic or new-age BS, yet it's true. I could never fix my spine, only do what I could to support it. Surgery, physical therapy, medications, Reiki, meditation, etc., these things could only provide the physical and emotional scaffolding, the structure to allow me to keep functioning. The problem was I kept trying to change it, to battle the disease and the pain, overcome it, conquer it — instead of being the best I could be, whatever that looks or feels like, and living in it — not through it or past it.

This is not a handbook about what you should or should not do, or yet another self-help book telling you that you have to fix something else in your life. It's just a story of what I went through. I believe that in the act of simply sharing our stories (both telling and listening), we can somehow reduce the pain in each of our lives, resting in the knowledge that we are completely and utterly supported in this world — and that gives us the courage to find our center, where we can accept and surrender to that peace.

In the first section of this book, I give you some of my history (both personal and medical). In the second section, I use my journal entries, with some narration, and the emails I sent to my support network, to share with you my process of healing after my last round of surgeries. These entries, written in the pain and joy I experienced as the process itself unfolded, tell my story better than I can recount it now. Some of my words will resonate with your own story; some will not. Either way, as I write this, I thank you from my heart for listening.

CHAPTER TWO

"Sorry" May be the Hardest Word, But "Starting" Ranks Right Up There

When you're not sure where to begin, most people agree it's best to start at the beginning. The tricky part is knowing where that beginning actually is and then facing the pressure of putting it down on paper.

When I was in college, I took a journalism class. It was the hardest class I ever took (my only B). It made Organic Chemistry look like recess. The professor was an editor at one of the city daily newspapers. His mission, I believe, was to smack us upside the head (figuratively, of course), until all the fluff came running out of our ears into the trash, leaving us with minds capable of sorting facts, prioritizing those facts and getting the information out within deadline. It was an 8:00 a.m. class — and if you remember anything about school, that in itself made the class brutal!

One of his many somewhat-sadistic exercises would be to give us a sheet of paper that had various facts about a story. We were given interview questions and answers, as well as all the background information we could possibly want and more. We had 15 minutes to write the story. If you didn't get the story written, some other ambitious reporter would get the front page . . . and you? You would get two inches on page 17 of the Life Section. Ready. Set. Go!

Given the pressure of that situation, most of us dealt with the white cow eating in the snow storm (aka, the blank page syndrome). And so he gave us a little trick to use. He said to start by simply writing, "Once upon a time . . ."

He told us that starting was the hardest part (it must have been one of his "soft" moments). He said the story would simply flow when we were no longer worried about the lead line. I've found life is like that. Most of us get wrapped up in our beginnings or the first line, or we constantly jump ahead to the next chapter of our story. It's hard to let the story play out in its own time, reveling in the telling, not the beginning or the ending.

Our professor said that once the story began to be developed, the beginning would be totally clear and we could rewrite it. I've used that trick in writing often in my life, and even passed it on to my son to help dispel writer's block. I also realized it extended beyond writing. And, to that end, I learned a few things along the way:

1. Getting started in doing anything is the hardest part. It requires us to change our lives in some way.

2. In most cases, some (or any) action is better than no action. Writing "once upon a time" is better than writing nothing at all. Standing by the sidelines does not accomplish anything — unless you wish to spend your life being a cheerleader and not a player. According to Buddha, "There are only two mistakes one can make along the road to truth; not going all the way, and not starting."

3. Other than murder, telling a woman she looks fat or wearing a fanny pack in public, there aren't a lot of things that can't be undone, redone or fixed in life. We can always go back and change the first line — change our thoughts, our words and our beliefs, and change our lives.

And so, here it goes. Maybe I won't need to go back and change this one.

Once upon a time . . .

CHAPTER THREE

Once Upon a Time …
And the Battle Begins

There was a girl who yearned with all her heart to make a difference in this world.

Blah. Blah. Blah. Okay, maybe I have to change it.

Once upon a time . . . there was a girl who searched the world over for the next battle to be won, only to find herself where she had been all along.

I was born in a little town in Maine. Okay, I admit it, Rumford, Maine. Home to one of the largest paper mills under one roof in the world. At one point, home to the 10th most polluted river in the world. Talk about an oxymoron — grow up in Maine and not have fresh air to breathe. Just the smell of rotten eggs. The adults would tell us it was the smell of our bread being buttered (in other words, food on our tables). No wonder I don't put butter on my bread these days.

Rumford is in southwestern Maine and rests in the valley of the White Mountains of New Hampshire. Not helping you geographically? Just a short ways from Mount Washington — you must have seen those bumper stickers that claim the car (not the persons) climbed Mount Washington, and the weather guy doing reports from the top of the mountain with icicles hanging off his beard while the wind and snow whip around him? Yeah, that's the place.

It's a typical working man's town, and although it sits in a beautiful landscape, the architecture in the town is not so aesthetic — sturdy, plain, functional, often run-down. The town sits on a hill and, of course, the church and better homes in town are at the top of the hill, with the mill houses at the bottom. We lived in one of those mill houses at the bottom of the hill, right next to the river. The house had a small footprint (just two or three rooms on each floor), but stood three stories high. There was just enough land around the house for a tiny flower garden on one side and a tight-fitting driveway on the other. In fact, all of us at some point ended up taking the electric meter off the house (and the mirror off the side of the truck) trying to pull into the driveway — that's how tight it was.

The best thing about the house was the beautiful lilac tree in the front — which I could smell each spring when I leaned out the window of my room on the top floor of the house. Most kids looked forward to the end of the school year. I looked forward to the lilac tree blooming.

When I go to Rumford now, I'm reminded of the movie, "Sweet Home Alabama." There's a scene in which Reese Witherspoon says, "You need a passport to come here." That's how I always felt. It's a different culture, different beliefs, different values and, probably most importantly, different fears.

I could swear my family has always thought they would absolutely disintegrate if they crossed the Piscatequa River Bridge, which is the border to New Hampshire on the south end on the way to Connecticut where I live now. Here, to go 30 minutes to the grocery store is no big deal. There, five minutes is too long. To go shopping in Lewiston (the big city!), just 45 minutes away, required months of planning and a really important reason — and there hardly ever was one. Leave the state of Maine? Horror of all horrors!

Life just doesn't exist beyond Rumford's immediate borders. Sometimes, I think that's not always a bad thing. Most of us get so caught up in the entire big wide world that we forget about the guy down the street who needs our help. The people in Rumford have a sense of community and neighborhood that doesn't exist anymore in too many places in this country. I think, in many ways, we could benefit by shrinking this world a bit.

But on the other side, it truly is "out of sight, out of mind." Apparently, the phone lines in Maine only run in one direction — incoming. Living about four hours away, I don't get calls to me unless someone is dead or dying. I don't exist for them on a daily basis unless there is a practical, logistical reason for them to contact me. After all, I'm the one who left. It's not conscious or with mal-intention (or at least my ego chooses to believe that). They just don't see anything beyond their normal daily lives — and those lives are full with the people who surround them in the immediate vicinity. Everyone else is extraneous. Unfortunately, because of my choices, that includes me.

I spent most of my childhood in Rumford working hard to excel — in school, music, art, whatever — conquering obstacles, creating higher and higher goals to overcome. I felt as though I was constantly searching and preparing for something else. There was more out there, I knew there was — greater battles to be fought and won, more to learn or experience. But in all my studying and reading and searching, I couldn't have told you who I was. I could only tell you what I had accomplished and what I was trying to accomplish next — past and future. Who I was at the moment was always a mystery, because I was already focused on who I would be tomorrow.

We were five kids in the family, with the three oldest a mere 20 months apart. Catholic triplets, they called us. My brother (Jimmy) was just nine months older than my sister (Susan), who is 11 months older than me. My sister's friends now routinely call her by her "grown-up" name, Sue; and my brother (now passed) hated it when I called him Jimmy, not Jim. But they are who they have always been to me as a child, and I never knew them in their new adult names — just as they never knew me.

When I would fight with my mother, and sometimes scream at her in anger that she didn't know anything about me, she would seem confused. After all, she knew what I had done yesterday and what I was going to do tomorrow. She knew everything about me, right? If I could see that she didn't know me, why couldn't I see that I didn't know myself?

The next two brothers who came after me were 3½ years and then another four years younger. I was called "Baby June" until I was a big girl of seven with two younger brothers (Joey and Jack). There were a lot of us, but I was lonely in a crowd. The brother next youngest to me, Joey, died in a fire at age seven. Another story, another time. Although he's been gone for a long time now, he has always had an impact on me. He was different, too, but he always seemed okay with it. Even so young, he knew himself and accepted himself completely.

When I really wanted to get Jimmy angry, I would tell him I was adopted. Most kids will taunt siblings by telling them that they were adopted. Not me. I would say that I was. Jimmy would get so mad and scream at me that it couldn't be true because I looked so much like Dad and him and my brothers. And he was right. Except for my sister, we were all the spitting image of my father.

And so I would say to my brother, "They did a great job picking out parents for me, didn't they?!" It would drive him nuts. I've often thought about that. In my fervent need to separate myself from a family in which I already felt different, my brother was really and truly scared by the concept that I wasn't one of them. I did enjoy driving him nuts, though.

I lived in a paradoxical situation. Dad was my champion in many ways. Since I was born on Father's Day, I was truly Daddy's Little Girl. He believed I could do anything.

Dad was born in Canada, came to the States, enlisted in the army and had seen some of the world. He chose to live in Rumford for his own reasons. He brought to me the understanding that there was a big world out there, well beyond the Maine borders. But it was kept almost as a secret. That was terribly confusing to me. On one hand, I was being encouraged to soar, to explore, to be great! On the other hand, the rest of the family was all about containment, staying put, being content where they were. I believed my Dad. But I wonder now if they were both right in some way. It's as difficult to comprehend now as it was then — how to be where you are, accept that place and find happiness, but at the same time, move forward and grow? One of life's riddles, I guess.

Dad told me anything was possible; I just had to want it badly enough. I could do anything in this world. If I failed, it was because I didn't want it enough to work for it.

Okay, many therapists reading this are rolling over, hands on their heads, groaning. Yes, it was incredible growing up with a parent who believed you were capable of anything. But pressure to perform — even pressure coming from absolute faith and belief and love — is still pressure, and the end result is the same: I could not fail. I had to hold strong. I couldn't crumple under the pressure.

I had to stay rigid. And so it began. The search to always find battles to be overcome, and the belief that overcoming those battles was what created and filled me.

On the outside, I wasn't a pretty girl. Luckily, my Dad's beliefs in me gave me focus and drive. I was fat, wore glasses, excelled academically and in many other schools would have been the nerd. I never had a date in high school, never went to the prom, never kissed a guy. But in our school, the smart kids were the popular ones. Although I didn't meet the physical specifications, being part of the smart group made me part of that popular group.

I was tall for my age and as a result didn't have especially good posture. Dad would follow me around with a stick with a nail on the end of it. When I didn't stand up straight, according to his military standards, he would poke me. It may not have been so bad if everyone hadn't laughed when he did it. Straight and strong, that was my goal.

What he and the others didn't understand was that, to me, I felt as though I WAS standing up straight. Working hard to change my posture when I got poked just didn't feel right — or natural. I didn't realize at the time that you can't possibly maintain something that just isn't you. At least, not for long. And certainly not without damage. At the time, I still believed I could do anything, change anything, overcome anything, be anything.

None of the humiliation mattered, though, because I always knew I would leave. In the end, I would overcome this as well. I never thought about the present day because I was always getting ready for the future when I could finally get away. I'm not saying it didn't hurt. I just knew I would leave it all behind someday. Now I wonder if you ever really do leave it behind.

My childhood and high school went by in a blur. I have few memories other than those I've shared here. Even the memories I do have feel as though they belong to someone else, like I've watched them in a movie. I really didn't exist in myself, except in my future dreams of who I would someday become — or, more correctly, what I would someday do.

Once upon a time . . . there was a girl who searched the world over for the next battle to be won, only to find herself where she had been all along.

CHAPTER FOUR

My Back-Breaking Battle
(No pun intended. Okay, small pun.)

I've told you a little about my past in the interest of starting at the beginning and helping you get a picture of how I arrived at this point. The picture of this woman whose only identity was tied up in doing rather than being; someone who looked at any situation — let alone a debilitating medical condition — as a battle to be won, and even constantly in search of the next battle, sword in hand, trying desperately to stand up straight and strong. Goodness, life was hard!

I did leave Rumford. And even now, I hardly ever go back — really only for weddings and funerals. When I left, I felt as though I had finally started my life. But while I couldn't describe my existence before then as "living," I also have to admit I really didn't start living when I left either. I still believed the grass would always be greener on the other side of the fence, so I never quite learned how to be happy in my own pasture.

What happened over the next 30 years didn't change things much, and so it won't add much here to go into detail about that now. To make an exhaustingly long story short, I did well in my career, lost 50 pounds, got married, had a son (Jason), got divorced and remarried (Peter), and started a second successful career. How's that for short? I experienced my share of struggles and faced each one valiantly. After all, that's how I did things. With my second marriage to Peter, in our first 18 months together, our family had seven operations (including my first two back surgeries), two broken bones, one catastrophic injury (my son fell off a horse and was bedridden for almost six months). My husband and I both lost our jobs. We had two car accidents and the engine in my car blew up. You think maybe something was trying to give me a clue about how I was facing obstacles? I was certainly getting enough practice!

My back pain began after my son was born, more than 25 years ago. I went from doctor to doctor and was diagnosed with everything from Lupus to Fibromyalgia to Rheumatoid Arthritis. I was even patted on the head and assured that all new mothers had back pain.

Eventually, I was told I had a mild curvature, but was assured that "scoliosis doesn't cause pain." (Yeah, right.) Adult onset is rare, so the doctors believed I'd had it since childhood, undiagnosed, and they didn't expect it to get worse at this point. Unfortunately, that was not the case.

With physical therapy, medication, improved overall fitness, a careful diet and massage, I worked hard to manage the progression of the curvature over the next 10 years. I also began to experience other medical problems which I later learned were, most likely, related to my diagnosis. At that point, though, after 10 years of fighting the disease, I was so crooked and in so much pain that my only option was surgery. I had done everything I could to overcome it and win — but it got me anyway.

I had my first surgery in 1999. I worked hard in physical therapy and did well for a little over a year. And then my back curved again — from a corrected 22 degrees (20 is normal) to over 60 degrees. Again, I did everything right. Again, it got me anyway.

A second surgery in 2001 fused most of my spine in an attempt to anchor the back with hardware and keep the curve from progressing again. This was followed by six months of agonizingly intense physical therapy and more medication. Only this time, I knew I needed to do something more. I had to beat this thing. I began doing meditation and eventually stopped all pain medication. I expanded my fitness program to include aqua therapy and saw big differences in my flexibility. Between the two, my pain and stress levels were manageable — for almost two years.

And then, one of the rods broke. Yes, a pencil-sized titanium rod, screwed into my spine, cracked and eventually completely separated. Why? The force of the scoliosis trying to curve the back? Who knows? No matter why,

I was looking at yet another surgery. This one carried uncertainty. If the back was fully fused, no new hardware would be put in. If not, I was looking at a repeat of the last big surgery.

It may seem odd, but I wasn't really scared. I had faith in my doctor and my physical therapist, and even more faith in myself. This was just one more thing to overcome, another battle in the war to win.

I pulled out all the stops. I practiced biological imagery meditations every day to picture the spine as snowy white, fused and healed. I practiced other meditations for pain and stress. I hired a personal trainer and worked with her three times each week for about two months before the surgery, not only to keep as much core strength as I could, but also to strengthen my legs and arms, which would have to work harder while my back was healing. I hired an aqua trainer to continue working with me on my mobility. I went to an osteopath and began a healing diet and supplement regimen. And the day before the surgery, I sent out an email to everyone I knew and asked them to take a moment the next day to stop and send up a prayer or a blessing for me. This was new for me. I had never called on other people to help when I had something to overcome. I always fought my battles alone.

This time, I was diligent and purposeful about every single thing I did and ate — and intent upon creating the perfect healing environment within my body. I was a true warrior, ready for battle.

CHAPTER FIVE

One More Time — My Own Version of the Hundred-Years War

The surgery went well and I did not need more hardware. Yay! I have no way of knowing if everything I did made a difference, but it sure made me feel like I was in control when I went into that operating room. In Jon Kabat-Zinn's Mindfulness Based Stress Reduction program, the concept of getting control is a fundamental teaching to reduce stress and pain. I have since learned that you must surrender to really attain control, but it worked at the time — for almost five years.

During that time, I worked hard to stay fit and even began a second career as a personal trainer. I especially enjoyed working with people who had back problems, because I felt I had much to offer. It was a rewarding job, but also tremendously demanding physically. It eventually took its toll on my body and my back began to break down. It's difficult to say if the very work that was helping to keep me fit was that which was destroying me . . . or if my back would have broken down even sooner had I not been a personal trainer. But now that I've been sidelined, I try to look at the experience with gratitude for having had the opportunity to, in some small way, help someone else. I neither regret it nor do I wish I could still do it. I am simply where I am right now, with the good, the bad and the ugly.

Let me go back a bit to fill in the holes about how I got to this point.

In January 2010, it became painfully (very painfully) clear that yet another surgery was imminent. We scheduled it for March. I got my affairs in order, made arrangements for temporary coverage of my clients (I planned to be out of work about a month) and ramped up or reinstituted many of the same things I had done last time. I felt confident because I knew what to expect: surgery, brace and physical therapy. I knew what pain and impairment levels to expect. I knew what the progression would be like. I knew how hard I would have to work. And I knew I would be better than before. So, what could go wrong?

More than I could ever have imagined.

One of the most important things I learned from all this is the value of creating and reaching out to a support system. Through my process, what began as emails to simply keep friends and family informed about what was happening became one of the most valuable tools in my recovery. And the responses I received were incredibly supportive and validating. These people in my life were like a circle of hands around me, holding me up while at the same time gently nudging me in the right direction. I could say anything to them and know it would never be judged and would be held in the utmost compassion. They listened to me patiently for more than a year! (There's a chance — a small one, mind you — that I may talk too much.)

With each round of emails sent out and responses back, I began to notice all the different kinds of support I had. Their responses were as different as the people sending them. Some found humor and tried to keep me upbeat. Some shared their stories of pain and hurt with me. Some responses were full of insight, ideas or approaches I hadn't considered. Some were religious or spiritual. And some could be counted on to tell me like it is, holding back nothing, making me face those truths. Others were expressions of simple love and compassion. I enjoyed them all, couldn't wait to receive them. I read them over and over and held on to them like a child holds on to a favorite Teddy bear. They comforted me, uplifted me, gave me strength and courage. With each one of their words, I could feel their arms around me, their hugs warming me and their smiles letting me know there was still much joy to be discovered.

These friends surrounded me and were an integral part of this journey. I'd like to introduce you to them here.

Renee, Sue M, Frank, Claudia, Laila, Shaunn, Bernice, Carmen S, Jill, Liz V, Nikki and Sue . . . former clients of mine, but more importantly, real friends. I could always count on them for their humor, their warmth and their reminder that I had value in their lives — that and an occasional glass of wine or two!

Michelle, Carmen H, Pat, George, Patty P and Allie . . . colleagues of mine at different times in my life. These vastly different people have several things in common: their constant support, dignity, quiet wisdom and willingness to listen. They soften my heart with their unconditional friendship.

Deanna . . . who came to my meditation groups and leads workshops of her own. Her gentle wisdom always resonates in my heart.

Jean, Linda, Dee, Eileen F, Kim, Ann, Liz B, Patty K, Patti and Carrie . . . women I met at a retreat led by Deanna. These women struck me with their bravery and their connectivity to one another. They all knew each other, but didn't know me. And they still warmly received me into their group. Over the last year, they have impressed me with their insights and the generosity of their love and friendship.

Eileen H and Paul . . . family of a former client who had passed away. Their gentle ways and soft spirits always leave me feeling incredibly valued and loved.

Brian . . . although shy with expressing his words, someone who is steadfast in his support and friendship. He may not like to talk much, but he is a really great listener!

Kimberly, Laurie, Leslie and Doris . . . four unbelievably beautiful women who approach spirituality in distinct ways: Laurie and her love for God; Kimberly with strength, knowledge and conviction; Doris with curiosity and a search for answers; and Leslie with hard work, dedication, humor and compassion from her own painful struggles. I met them all in different places over the years while we were all struggling to find our way along the path. Their insights constantly amaze me and their warmth and love is never ending.

Jack . . . my dear, sweet younger brother who works so hard to keep me connected to our family. His continued love and quiet dignity have always been a source of support for me.

Debbie . . . a friend from a long time ago (from my former corporate life) who has witnessed many of my "transitions" and remains a big part of my present. Always genuine of heart, her simple way of giving and expressing her love and her loyal friendship are constants in this journey of transformation.

Carolyn . . . who was having a baby and then dealing with a newborn and a two-year old when this all started. And yet, this wonderful friend still found time to make sure I knew she was there for me. Her gentle love and quiet wisdom are great gifts in my life. We have shared laughter, tears, joys and sorrows — and occasionally a little wine — on the beach near her house.

Gwen . . . who has since passed. We went through many struggles together. I will always miss her friendship, gentle spirit and "slight" fixation for chocolate!

Cheryl . . . a spiritual guide in my life and wonderful friend. Her gentleness of spirit, simple grace and wisdom have helped to lead me to this place of peace.

Dory . . . my long-term mentor and gifted spiritual counselor who (thankfully) has never held back in telling me what I needed to face. She has always had a way of getting me to open my eyes "underwater." She has been my touchstone for many years, someone I come back to time and time again for guidance and wisdom, and I am thankful that she led me to Cheryl and Richard. With the warmth, honesty and encouragement of her nurturing spirit, she has always been there to help me face my truths and direct me onward.

Richard . . . a dear, dear teacher and, if possible, even more dear friend. He embodies the wisdom and intuition of the true spiritual guru and has often known me better than I knew myself. His quiet, constant love, guidance and friendship are instrumental in helping me along this path. He is my spiritual home.

I owe all these people my eternal gratitude. They and my wonderful husband, *Peter*, gave me the strength and encouragement I needed to live fully in and through this journey. Without their love and support, this story would not have existed.

In the next section of this book, the emails I wrote to these beautiful friends, along with some narration, become the vehicle for telling my story. I've included their incredibly supportive and validating responses as well. As you read, it is my hope that their words, not only mine, will leave you feeling as though you are part of the story. May you feel the same warm caress of their support and compassion, and may our words speak to you with the unconditional love we intend.

And so, the story begins again — this time with a vastly different ending.

Finding Center — Crooked or Not, Here I Come!

Thursday, March 11, 2010

Today, I have my last round of clients before tomorrow's surgery. I hurt. A lot. My clients can see the pain on my face, something I have tried to keep hidden for many months now. But I no longer have the energy to hide. I can hardly stand up. Everyone told me to take today off. But I couldn't do that. I won't be making any money for the next month. Besides, the last thing I need is to spend this final day alone at home with nothing to do but think about tomorrow.

I just have to get through today. *Keep going. Just one more client. Stay upbeat. They all expect it from you. You'll be back in just a month. In a back brace, but you'll be back. One foot in front of the other. You can do this.*

Tomorrow, I will begin the process of healing again. The good news is I know what to expect. The bad news is I know what to expect. I'm not looking forward to the surgery or the recovery, but I know I can do it since I've done it before. I'm not nervous about the surgery, but there is a part of me that just doesn't want to do it, even though I know it's necessary and, in the end, my pain level will be better.

I feel as though I'm holding myself tightly, just hanging on until tomorrow. I've done everything I can to get ready. There is a level of calm in me, but for some reason there is some sadness too. I don't know why. Maybe I'm just tired. Tired of being in pain. Tired of pushing. Tired of fighting. Am I afraid I don't have the fight in me necessary to get through this? The recovery was so hard last time. I'm too old to do this again. No, no, no! I'll fight. I'll get through it.

I'm trying to put aside my visions — or lack of them. I don't understand why I can't visualize my life after the surgery when I try to meditate on the outcome, imagining my spine healthy and my life back to normal. I'm trying not to panic about what that means. Richard, my friend and teacher, says it's because my life as I know it will be different after the surgery, and I don't have a frame of reference to see it or comprehend it yet. It makes me somewhat uncomfortable, but I think I'm just too tired and in too much pain to care about the outcome anymore. What will be, will be. I'll deal with it.

Tonight will be easy. No dinner tonight. Finish the laundry. A little meditation. Try not to think too much. Bed early. Tomorrow will be easy, too. After all, I'll be sleeping through it. I hope my doctor is getting to bed early, too. I want him as well rested as possible!

But first, my email call-out to my friends for energetic support . . .

March 11, 2010 Email

Re: Could sure use your prayers!

Hello, friends!

As most of you know, I am going in for back surgery tomorrow, 3/12. I'm really sorry if I haven't spoken with you directly yet. It came up faster than I expected. The surgery is scheduled for 7:30 a.m. and is expected to last 10 hours. I will be in the hospital for five to seven days, home for four weeks, in a brace for three months and in physical therapy for six months.

But by the end of the year, I will be better than new!

And so I have a favor to ask . . . at some point tomorrow if you wouldn't mind stopping for a moment to think of me and send up a prayer, blessing, mantra, mental hug — whatever your beliefs are. I am completely non-denominational when asking for energetic support!

Thanks, everyone! My husband, Peter, will send you an email (it will come from my email address) to let you know all is well. And then, once I am home and coherent, I will plan to connect with each of you.

June

My email brought many responses . . . and I am overwhelmed by the love and support.

You have been on my mind an exponential amount as of late. I can now see why . . . As always you will be in my thoughts and I will definitely be sending my prayers. Renee

Of course I will be thinking of you and praying for you. You will do great!!! Sue

You will be in my prayers. I have been thinking of you since the day before I got your email. Good luck, sweetie. Lots of love, Leslie

As always I wish you health and happiness. My prayers will be with you. Brian

I sent out some healing energy to you this morning . . . hope you received it! Eileen H

I'm sending you good thoughts . . . and asking the angels to watch over you. Debbie

I've been keeping you in prayer and know His hands are upon you through this. Sorry you have to go through this, but I can see your beautiful smile as you overcome once again! Be blessed, beautiful friend. Laurie

You know my energy and comfort is with you. Think of me, and feel safe. For you will be. It's not in my power that comfort comes . . . but in your heart that you choose to be here . . . and know you have the power to make it so. Trust in your own Divine Essence, and that it alone knows your highest choices . . . your greatest expression . . . yet to be told. And it is in that desire to tell your "truth" that the power to keep you safe and vibrant is realized! I will be there, in dreams and the awakening. Make the most of the journey. See the smile that greets you . . . See you tomorrow, Richard

I can sleep tonight, knowing I am so lovingly supported. I have nothing to fear. Goodness, I'm tired.

Friday, March 12, 2010

The drive to the hospital is going by in a blur. Literally, since I don't have my contacts in. I can't see a thing, and I don't strain to try. It's sort of pleasant. Makes me feel like I'm in a warm cocoon, all wrapped in cotton wool. It gives me the impression that I'm a little separate from what's happening, like I'm not really experiencing it.

I don't feel like talking, which is fine because Peter is always okay with not talking. I'm just waiting. There is no agitation; in fact, I feel rather calm. I have a great doctor (Dr. Mohr) and I trust him completely. There is nothing to be concerned about. Everything is in place and set. I'm ready. This is the part where I don't have to do anything. My part's easy; I just sleep.

I've packed books and meditation CDs for my stay in the hospital. I'm almost looking forward to the down time. Almost, but not quite. There are certainly better ways to get down time. I must really need a vacation.

Peter tries to keep me distracted with humor. I know that it's his way of dealing with stress, so I go along, even though I just feel like being quiet. With each joke, it's like he's handing me a rose and saying, "I love you." He makes everyone around him feel lighter, and we let any unspoken concerns slide away with the laughs, at least for a little while.

They take me into the pre-op area pretty quickly. There's still plenty of time before the scheduled surgery. I guess there's a lot of prep for a 10-hour surgery. As much as I love Peter and appreciate his love, I hope he will leave me some alone time before they take me into the operating room. I feel like I need to just go inside for a bit. Actually, I'd like to do that now, but I've suddenly become wildly popular with nurses, residents, anesthesiologists — hospital bracelet, IVs, blood work, questions, more questions. How many times do I have to admit my birthday (and therefore, my age)?!

Through it all, Peter keeps up the humor and the staff is happy that he has, at least temporarily, taken away the somber mood of the pre-op area. He makes me laugh, too, and I can admit that it helps.

Dr. Mohr comes in just before game time. I can see the gentleness of spirit in his eyes and hear the compassion in his words. He is an oddity — a caring doctor. He always makes you feel like you are his only patient. I am confident to put myself in his hands. I take a deep breath and he assures Peter and me that we will get through this together.

Peter stays with me until it's time, which is okay even though I didn't get my alone time. I would much rather have him with me, after all.

I decline the pre-op medications of Versed and Valium, preferring to go into the operating room clear and conscious. Maybe since my vision is blurred, leaving me with that cocoon feeling, I'm able to surrender a little. I kiss Peter, smile and say good-bye. I'm okay. I'm ready.

Saturday, March 13, 2010

Before the surgery, I had already composed an email for
Peter to send out as an update to my friends. (He hates
to write.) It was set up on my computer, so that all he
had to do was hit "send." Unfortunately, things did not
go as planned. I had dural leaks, which meant I was
leaking spinal fluid. Dr. Mohr attempted to repair it as
best as possible and now it was a case of wait-and-see.
When I first woke up, I could not lift my right leg and I
felt disassociated, as though my arms weren't connected
to my brain. I had difficulty reaching for water and
talking coherently. I was scared, but felt too ill to really
comprehend or express the fear. I really believed this
couldn't happen to me. Really, everything was still going
to be okay, wasn't it?

And so, Peter had to write his own email.

Emailed by Peter, March 13, 2010

Hello, everyone!

This is Peter, June's husband. June asked me to let you know how her surgery went. After 14 hours of surgery on Friday, June spent most of the day on Saturday sedated and on her back, as the doctor wanted no movement for the first 24 hours to try to heal the dural leaks she experienced from the surgery. This morning, she saw glimpses of consciousness and daylight and is doing fine. It will just be a long, long road to recovery.

June asked me to thank all of you for your thoughts, prayers and best wishes. She will be in touch in the next couple weeks.

Peter

And Peter's email brought many responses and continued prayers . . .

Thank you, Peter. Love and blessings for June's healing! Cheryl

I was so relieved to hear that June is doing well. She is such a wonderful, thoughtful, talented person, and has a mental strength and confidence that is awesome considering the pain she's been through! During our physical training sessions, we have had many conversations on a variety of topics including science, medicine and politics, and her knowledge and acuity has been a delight to me! I am an 85-year-old retired widower with an extensive background in physics and science, but with few people to share my knowledge with. Being with June has not only helped me physically, but has given me a great, much-needed mental boost as well! Tell her she has my prayers, and I wish her a speedy uncomplicated recovery! Frank

Thanks, Peter. Please send June loving energy from me from afar, and I hope she is surrounded by caring friends and family to help her with the recovery. I have so much confidence in her healing energy. I know she will recover as well as possible. With love, Leslie

I am humbled by their love and kindness.

Monday, March 15, 2010

I continue to have difficulty lifting my leg or using my arms, and I am in great pain, having to lie flat on my back without moving. My fear has not yet bubbled to the surface, maybe because I still refuse to believe this new reality. But I know I'm really not well because I haven't cared a bit that my hair is tangled and greasy, and I can't remember if I've brushed my teeth. Dr. Mohr and his residents, as well as a stream of nurses, come to check on me regularly. And every time I manage to open my eyes, Peter is there waiting for me. But it all goes by in a blur. My mind is hazy and my brain seems disconnected. I can barely string two sentences together. The morphine may have something to do with that, but I'm guessing that leaking spinal fluid into my brain doesn't help either.

And so, after four days of hoping for the dural leaks to heal on their own, Dr. Mohr recommends another surgery to repair them. I accept this without emotion. I'm just there, going through the motions, a rag doll. I am completely reliant on his and Peter's judgment, and I trust them. I can't think and, for the first time in my life, I don't even try.

I feel no resentment about being so dependent. There is no fight in me at all. Also for the first time in my life, I accept things just as they are. I am exactly where I am. I willingly surrender.

I sign the papers with a shaky hand, my signature barely legible. It doesn't matter. Surgery is scheduled for tonight. It should only take a couple of hours. I will be better tomorrow.

Wednesday, March 17, 2010

Emailed by Peter.

June asked me to thank you all for your emails and calls of support. She appreciates knowing you are all there supporting her!

As far as her recovery goes, during June's first surgery she encountered some dural tears (go look that one up!), which caused a leaking of spinal fluid into her brain. This causes extreme nausea and headaches, and she is not recovering as well as she should. The bottom line is that June had to undergo a second surgery last night, and she is basically at ground zero with respect to recovery time. She will probably be in the hospital for the upcoming week, and probably won't be up for visitors or making calls for some time yet.

Again, she appreciates your support. The best thing you can do right now is to give her a little time to recover and get her strength back, so please be patient in hearing back from her. Of course, if you absolutely feel compelled that you must do something to help, our mortgage is due on the first of the month. I know we would both appreciate that!

———

Ever the joker . . . when I read Peter's email later, I knew he was concerned. Thankfully, I didn't know it before the surgery. I would have been more worried myself. His humor, though, lightened the worries of my friends.

Love the part about the mortgage — very adorable! And I bet you're only half kidding! I'm glad to receive the update on June. Thanks so very much. Dory

Continuing to send love and prayers. Carolyn

Thank you for the update, although I am sorry to hear the bad news. You're both in my thoughts every day. I know you will let us know when June is ready for some communication and I look forward to that. In the meantime, I hope she's not worried about work. I'll do my best to keep Jill and Liz in great shape until she's ready to return! Allie

Thanks for letting us know about June's second surgery. Sorry to hear that she had to go through that. It sounds like a very painful process. Please give her our best and keep in touch. As for the mortgage, we'll see what we can do! Take care. Eileen H and Paul

Thursday, March 25, 2010

It's amazing! I'm actually starting to feel human. I asked Peter to bring in my laptop so I can send out the emails myself and resume my journaling. He is quite glad to relinquish the responsibility since writing is not his thing.

———◦———

March 25, 2010 Email

Re: Will the third time be the charm?

Hello, all!
It's really June this time, not Peter!

Although I am sending you this email directly, I am unfortunately still in the hospital. I believe you all heard about the second surgery (Tues, 3/16, a little over four hours) which required fixing some dural leaks and relocating a couple screws. Yes, I really did have a screw loose! It was a difficult recovery, requiring three more transfusions (total of seven since I've been here) and the need to lie completely flat for 72 hours afterward. Still, things were looking good and I was able to get fitted for my brace — a remarkable piece of "support" that requires at least 20 minutes and a 500-calorie workout to put on!

And last Friday, I began walking laps around the nurses' station on the floor — what a sight — johnnie flowing out (sorry, no flashing), cute little knee-high compressions socks, no makeup, the shiny metal of the brand-new walker! You can bet my dance card was full! Except for some incredible numbness, pain and weakness in my legs and my degenerating dignity, I was steadily improving.

Body systems, however, did not all return to normal as quickly as we all would have liked, and I was still not feeling well. At this point, the drama really began to heat up when a renegade resident put through a discharge order on me without discussing it with my doctor. You can imagine the resident took a beating, as my doctor took on those endearing qualities of a highly motivated mother hen!

I have not seen this resident since, and have heard much gossip and giggling about it from the other residents and nurses.

In the meantime, I have been running a low-grade temp, with chills and sweats, as well as a lot of drainage from the incision. So now I am scheduled for a third surgery tonight. This procedure should only last about a half hour, and the intent is to open up the wound, flush it out, culture the drainage and proceed with antibiotics as needed. They will watch the incision for another day, but then that means I should be able to go home on Saturday.

Time for my nap now!

My heartfelt thanks to all of you for your notes, calls, visits, cards, flowers and the sincere warm wishes of your friendships. Just knowing you are out there has made it easier to deal with the challenges.

Miss you all and look forward to rejoining your worlds soon!

June

P.S. And for those of you who know me really well — I sold three of my meditation CDs while in here!

This was a time of increasing optimism for me, even while facing a third surgery. I didn't yet understand the ramifications of this upcoming procedure, and I was feeling so good about having come this far (especially compared to how I felt after the first surgery) that I figured I could overcome anything. I knew it was possibly an infection, but I was incredibly nonchalant about another surgery and the aftermath. I should have felt like a punching bag at this point — recovering from an initial difficult procedure, experiencing severe complications and now feeling increasingly sick with a possible infection? But I seemed to just take the next blow without it actually affecting me. Maybe I was numb. I could see the concern in Dr. Mohr's face and I found myself wanting to comfort him, reassuring him that I trusted his judgment and would do whatever he needed me to do. The responses from my friends reflected this optimism, and they were all envisioning me recovered, home and getting back to life. Their messages carried me through the next hurdle. They could see a positive future and, through their eyes, so could I.

Wow! I am stunned. Good God, the third time WILL be the charm. Thanks so much for the update, and I love the funny parts! You are something else! While you may think your dignity factor is declining, I think you're amazing. I'm keeping you in the light and hope this next one goes smoothly and you can get on home. Best to you and lots of love! XX, Leslie

Thanks for the update, but I'm so sorry you're having all that trouble! And I'm not surprised you sold three CDs while you were in there! When you are up to it, I'll buy you lunch. Maybe a glass of wine will help you recover. I hope you have a speedy recovery! Brian

Love your spirit!!! Continuing to pray for you and let this be the last! Quick healing! Laurie

The greatest wish for you of all is to heal well and complete this lesson, so that you may be free to again pursue your dreams and grace us all with more of the essence of you in all your Divinity! In the meantime, I continue to be there for you, in spirit and humanity. We have much to talk about when you are settled into the new you. Blessings and love. Richard

Sounds like you are running a hospital marathon. What a journey! And I am so glad to hear that you are in your final stretch and will be released after some final "touch up surgery." Lots of light and healing energy to support your recovery in the weeks to come. Blessings and well wishes. Doris

My thoughts and prayers are with you, my friend. Love, Carolyn

I am so sorry about the problems you've had with your surgery and recovery, and I am so amazed at your upbeat attitude despite all your setbacks! I've told you in the past that I consider you to be one of the strongest, well-focused women I have ever met but you have exceeded even that! I wish I had a tenth of the strength and will and courage that you so naturally possess. You are a remarkable woman. Keep up the good work and know you are always in my prayers and thoughts. Frank

Sounds like you have had a rough time of it. Working in this field, I know about all the complications of surgery and it sounds like you are experiencing all of them. I am glad to hear from you — that is a positive sign and it will only get better from here. The warm weather and sunshine is coming and that can cure all our moods. I wish you the best. If you need anything, let me know. Stay positive! Claudia

I had no idea that you were undergoing such stress . . . please know that I am very glad to hear you are on the mend and will continue to pray for your well-being. I just finished reading about an African "miracle" response to a prayer, tears in my eyes and I KNOW, as I always have, that which we request in sincere need will always be addressed, even if we can't see at the moment how appropriately so! Maintain your peaceful core. It will never fail you. Liz B

Speedy recovery and much white light coming your way! Peace, Deanna

Yikes . . . you have had quite the journey! I am glad you can have such a great sense of humor about it all! When you are feeling ready, I will be happy to do some reflexology at your home for you! Hope things are getting better with each second. This has definitely been good practice for living life as a journey and not a destination! Michelle

I wish you every blessing as you continue to heal. May you find many moments of peace and clarity as you move forward. Cheryl

Let me know when you are home. As you know, I have been patiently waiting for the opportunity to barge into your house and park myself next to you and bring you junky, gossipy magazines and maybe some chocolate. After all, you are only five miles away and chocolate does not melt on the way there. It sometimes disappears for other reasons, though . . . :) Take VERY GOOD care. Gwen

Tuesday, March 30, 2010

Re: Home at Last!

Hello, all!
First of all — thank you for all your notes of well wishes and support. Today is the first day I have opened my laptop since sending the last update, and you can't imagine how much your words and thoughts helped me.

Secondly, I apologize for not responding to each of you individually, and hope you'll forgive me for this broadcast approach for a little while longer.

I am finally home from the hospital. I got home late Saturday night. The third surgery ended up lasting a little over two hours. My doctor was assisted by the hospital's doctor for infectious disease (Dr. Dieckhaus) — and yes, I have one of those horrible, nasty, hospital-borne infections. So the situation, ongoing care and treatment are a little more than I expected. Saturday, at the hospital, I had a consult with Dr. Dieckhaus who said that there was definitely something growing in the cultures they took, but they couldn't yet identify the specific bacteria. I was immediately put on Vancomycin (an IV antibiotic that kills everything, much like chemo does) and was told I would have to have two IV doses each day for six weeks. I couldn't leave the hospital until so late that day because they had to get that second dose in for the day. I had a temp of 101 when I was discharged, and I didn't think they were going to let me go. But apparently no one told my doctor, so I got to go home!

The nurse brigade started arriving on Sunday. One to clean my dressing and look after general care; another to get me started and trained on giving myself the IV treatment. (As I type this, I am hooked up right now to my IV, affectionately referred to as the "Bubble" because it looks like a ball.) The Bubble is dangerous stuff, with potential damage to my hearing, kidneys, liver and heart. Nurses arrive each day, and PT is expected to start today as well. I had blood work this morning (and will get it every week, minimally) to check my levels.

I am sure I will get through this as well — some people will do anything to get more time off, right? But I will be honest and say that I am very tired and don't really feel well. I am getting around okay with my brace, although still relying on a walker and a wheelchair because of the pain in my legs and overall fatigue. But, although today is not as good as yesterday, both days are much better than last week!

I get moments when I feel good and I want to do some work — write new meditations or outline some new workshops. I get lots of great ideas and can't wait to put them in place. I try to look forward and see what all this will do to change both my practice and me, and I try to put some positive structure around it.

But mostly I realize it's not the time to do even that right now. All I really have the energy for is to be exactly where I am. This is truly a lesson for being in the moment — a very harsh one, but a good one nonetheless. I don't look at things in terms of six weeks of IV treatments or three months in the brace anymore. I look at things on a daily basis, even a minute-by-minute basis, deciding what I need to do right now to feel better physically, emotionally and spiritually.

(Of course, that excludes the UConn Women's games — I do plan for those!)

I am sorry that I have not been able to be there for any of you right now. (Carolyn — congrats on the baby!) But I am settling into this for now and trusting in the power of all of you to keep sending me energy and love to help me heal. Not everything can be muscled through, and not everything needs to be a struggle. Sometimes you just have to surrender with complete knowingness and trust that it will all come out the way it's intended. I am putting down my sword and hoping I can borrow all of yours for a little while. It is your faith in me that helps me to keep faith in myself.

I will try to reach out to each of you over the next week or so. Feel free to call if you'd like. Anytime after

10:30 a.m. is great, except between 3–6 p.m. That is naptime and I'm getting quite fond of it!

Thanks, again! Blessings to each and every one of you!
Love,
June

I was trying really hard to settle in, and yes, it was a tremendously hard lesson about living in the moment. I was really too sick to do anything else. I still believed I would come out on top, but I was beginning to accept the possibility that I really didn't control the hows and whys.

As usual, the responses to my update brightened my spirits and my day. Some were serious, some funny. I was grateful for the connection from all of them. Many people remarked on how I was "inspiring" them; and yet, their words of love and support inspired me to keep going.

> *My continued thoughts and prayers are with you. You are an amazing woman. Such strength. Sending you warm light and love. Carolyn*

> *Sending much love! Yes, keep supporting the moment. The other stuff will follow. You need you right now. Those who love you will understand your need to focus on you. Love, Kimberly*

Sounds like you are on quite the journey! No need to try to be a hero. Taking care of yourself is paramount right now. Do only what brings you comfort. Life should not be lived with a sword. I like your statement of how you have put yours down. Congratulations — a great shift for you! See if you can leave it where it is — life is definitely not meant to be muscled through — anywhere. Wishes and oodles of healing and love to you, sweetie! Dory

May you drop in to a balance of allowing yourself to heal and working with inspiration. Every blessing. Cheryl

Wow, talk about being put through a wringer! Sorry to hear that you have to go through all of this. Keep up the positive thoughts/state of mind and focus on one day at a time. You are a strong person and will persevere. And like you said, each day and week will be better than the last. Jill

I'm so sorry you have to go through this huge ordeal. Thankfully, it sounds like you have a great attitude and your sense of humor is fully intact. Sue M

So glad to hear you are back home and a mere five miles away! I would offer to bring you some chicken soup, but not sure you want that from a vegetarian! But I am willing to try . . . and in the spirit of Easter coming soon, I'd be willing to hop on over with soup, chocolate or anything else. The only promise you need to make is to not even brush your hair — since buddies do not try to gussie themselves up for friends when they are feeling yucky. Love, Gwen

Sending you lots of love and healing energy. A health crisis can be trying, but it can also be most enlightening. It breaks everything away that we normally cling to for identity. All the unconscious business of our daily lives. All the ways of planning for the next moment, for tomorrow, and not living in the now. It sounds like a great opportunity to practice just that and listen to your body and heal. Rest, rest, rest and may your body heal and recover. Big hug, Doris

I'm so sorry to hear that you have to deal with an infection on top of everything else. I tried to send some good energy from my yoga class last night. I hope you received it and that you're feeling a little better today! Hang in there. You're very strong and I'm sure you'll get through this. Eileen H

My heart goes out to you. You have been in my thoughts non-stop since you last wrote to us all. Please know that your journey — and you — continue to be an inspiration. Debbie

Hope this note finds you able to at least enjoy the spring weather! I'm sure you're being the perfect patient

☺. *I'm thinking of you and sending you positive energy. I'd give you advice about living in the moment . . . but . . . as you know, I'm always in a hurry! I hope each day is a bit better than the last. Think of you often . . . Liz V (And Liz couldn't resist snitching on her daughter-in-law, Jill.) P.S. I don't think Jill is working out as often as she should!* ☺

At home, each day seemed to blur into the next. I slept a lot and was really too sick to do more than that. I think that in some ways being ill took over some of the pain. I wasn't taking much for pain medicine because it just made me feel even more ill. Although I wasn't doing anything all day, I wasn't bored. For the first time in my life, I was existing without being worried about being productive. I was even too sick to fight.

Wednesday, April 7, 2010

Re: Good news!

Hello, all!
Well, I got some good news this week! The cultures came back on the infection, and if you had to pick the best one to have, I got it. It is apparently the baby version of MRSA and is normally sensitive to antibiotics. So Dr. Dieckhaus changed my medication to Oxacillin and I am hooked up to a pump 24/7, which dispenses the meds every four hours. The good news is that it is supposed to shave a week off the treatment time. The pump is designed to be worn as a fanny pack — but I simply cannot, will not, do not do fanny packs! I have not yet degraded that far! Besides, with the size of the brace, it would be like Santa Claus wearing a fanny pack! I must leave myself some dignity!

I had to go to the Infusion Center at the hospital to get the first dose of the new medicine. The Infusion Center is located at the Cancer Treatment Center. Everyone there was so caring and compassionate, and it certainly went a long way toward eliminating any self pity. There is much truth to the saying, "I cried because I had no shoes until I met a man who had no feet." And it didn't matter to the staff that I was only there for an antibiotics infusion. It was so nice to see such incredible kindness. They couldn't do enough to make sure I was comfortable. Their caring went a long way toward making me feel better. What an incredible group of people!

I went from there to the spinal doctor, who was very happy with how I was moving, my pain levels and the way the incision was healing. And his staff is so nice, they were genuinely happy that I was doing well. My X-rays look like I was hit by a truck — which then backed up over me twice more. It's not pretty, but it works.

Each day seems a little better. With the change of medicine, I've felt a little sick again, but I'm sure that will abate. I'm moving more and more, and today my goal is to get to the end of the driveway and back! And no, it's not a short driveway!

Clothing is interesting — I'm wearing my husband's sweatpants or shorts, which make me look like Erkle (not sure how he spelled it). Very sexy. The T-shirts are just as bad. But I know it's temporary, and I believe we can handle anything if we know it's going to end.

I miss everyone, but I am staying with my resolve to settle into an awareness of where I am and what comes out of it. Thank you, all, for going through this with me!

Love,

June

I was trying hard to be the upbeat warrior again. Positive outlook. It's not so bad. I can get through this . . . I really only half believed it. I'm sure it's what I needed to believe. But I had myself fooled, and many of my friends.

I cannot imagine all that you are going through. You are amazing to keep such an upbeat outlook!!! As for your outfits, a little bling always helps!!!. You are in my thoughts and prayers! Patty K

Everything sounds positive! I am glad to hear you are improving daily. May your total recovery be swift! Patti

Hey, Beautiful June! Always great to hear from you and so glad your healing is coming along! God bless! Laurie

Dearest June. I am holding you in my awareness and wishing you every blessing! Much love, Cheryl

I've said it to you before and I really meant it — you are one amazing woman! To have to go through what you've been going through without losing your focus or faith in the outcome . . . boggles my mind! Get well soon. I miss you! Frank

I'm so glad to hear that you're doing better!!! I don't blame you for not using the fanny pack . . . not a good look! Eileen H

You have my blessings and my prayers. Dee

So, since you're doing so well, I guess that means I'll see you Tuesday for my workout! Don't worry about the "sexy" thing for now . . . it comes from the inside. And don't lose any more weight or I will force feed you chocolate cake — that's if I don't get to it first! Sue M

I love that you have such optimism and humor! Keep up the effort and I'll keep you in my thoughts and send you white light. ☺ Kim

You are certainly a gutsy lady and I commend you on your positivity in the face of such a hard fight! God bless you as you mend and give you strength which will turn out to be your inspiration as you go forward. I have the feeling that you are turning lemons into lemonade! Eileen F

I can feel your courage and upbeat gentleness. Blessing to you and your family. Linda

So all things considered . . . you are on the road to recovery! And yes, I have been working out, as I heard my "mother-in-law" threw me under the bus! Be sure to give her extra push-ups when you return! Jill

Hey, Sis! I'm glad you're finally home, but so sorry you had to go through all that to get there! I'm glad you still have your sense of humor about you! Not to say that I'm all that religious anymore, but I've been talking to God a lot lately. I'm trying my best to send you some positive energy to help you recover. I'm glad you're in good spirits, and if I know you, there's no way you are going to let it beat you! In the meantime, listen to the doctors and be a good patient! By the way, I'm really jealous of that 3–6 p.m. thing you've got going!!! Love, Jack

I am so sorry that you've had to deal with all of this! I guess it's true that we really don't know how much we can handle until we're faced with it. God bless. Carrie

A very appropriate response from Carrie. Unfortunately, I didn't know I would have so much more to handle.

Tuesday, April 13, 2010

Re: It's a dance — step forward, step back . . . and then forward again!

Hello, all!

Last week, I mentioned that I was fortunate enough to have gotten the "baby" version of the family of staph infections and that the doctor had opted to change my medication to Oxycillin, which has fewer potentially dangerous side effects. Unfortunately, within three days of the change, I was very sick again and my temp was rising. I was also getting increasing pain in my right leg. Needless to say, I was very quickly put back on Vancomycin, which means I'm back to the IV twice a day. I am now feeling much more alert and normal (whatever that means), although the pain in my leg is horrendous. It's possible that the infection spread to the bone in my leg — not unusual, but nothing to panic about — even if it did, the Vanco will vanquish anything!!!

I am pretty much OFF pain medicines, except for Neurontin at night for nerve pain. After the surgeries, my legs (and other parts) were numb. Now the feeling is coming back. Unfortunately, when nerves start to wake up again, they are like newborn babies — colicky newborn babies . . . colicky newborn babies that need a diaper change! You get my point . . . Just a challenge to my meditation skills . . . I may kill the bird that keeps pecking non-stop on our solarium windows, but the pain in my leg is subsiding nicely . . .

Tomorrow, I am getting a brand new gadget — an electronic bone stimulator! Doesn't that sound exciting? Evidently, they hook these electrodes up to each side of my incision and it's connected to some sort of power pack that is the size of a cell phone. I carry it around all day and every so often, it sends an electronic impulse to my spine. So if I stutter when I'm talking to you, you'll know why. Who knows, getting zapped could be the most fun I've had in a while!!!

I drove yesterday for the first time! Yay! It was pretty exciting to get some independence back! My leash-length isn't too far yet, but it's a start! Maybe soon I'll be able to meet you somewhere — for a walk, lunch, just to talk. Let me check . . . yes, my social calendar has a few openings . . .

As you can see, I'm trying to celebrate the small steps. And this whole process has been a dance of forward then back — but it always goes forward again. Even the fact that I'm ready for the bone stimulator is a good sign. And although my nerves are screaming, it's not forever, and there are so many more people dealing with more permanent pain.

One of the things I've noticed lately that I think is a bit strange is that some of the things I used to enjoy hold no interest for me. I have always been a "House" (TV show) fan and now I can't get through an episode. Thriller/mystery stories (John Grisham, James Patterson, etc.) leave me sleeping by the third page. And horror of all horrors — the thought of pizza does nothing for me. (And when you live a mile from Willington Pizza, that's no small thing!) It's like I'm becoming a blank page just waiting for the inspiration to paint the next exciting "stuff." I'm taking walks, or just sitting outside, not really thinking about much, just noticing and appreciating. The rest will come.

What has not changed is how much I miss my clients — who are really and truly my friends — and I continue to thank all of you for being a part of my life and for allowing me to share yours. You are my core, and everything builds from there. And don't get too excited — that doesn't mean I'm going soft on you! I just may practice on that bird . . . !

I WILL see you all soon!

With love and gratitude,

June

I continued to have setbacks, but kept that smile on my face. It must have taken a lot of energy to do so . . . My friends responded in kind, happy that I could stay so positive.

I hope that all of this will soon be over and you will be back to torturing your dear clients who are getting fatter by the hour! Love, Laila

May your "blank page" become filled with much joy and laughter. I look forward to hearing more stories of your road to recovery, or should I say your road to the new June! Carrie

You are truly a peaceful warrior! Peace, blessings and healing to you! Cheryl

Dear Wonderwoman! I continue to be more and more impressed at your mental strength and positive outlook despite setbacks that would drive most people to despair! You seem to have become a portable experimental laboratory for exotic treatments! As usual, wonderwoman conquers all. Give yourself enough time to heal. The world will still be there when you're ready to tackle it! Frank

I'm frustrated for you! If your email is any indication of how your mood is, you are truly a strong individual.

Here's to making the best of difficult situation! Praying for you to recover soon! Sue M

You are amazing! You'll be dancing a jig in no time! Until then, a fox trot or stroll is AOK! Keep up the good work! Patty K

You have gone and are going through so much! My thoughts and prayers are with you. You are such an inspiration. I believe that attitude makes the difference and I see you have a wonderful one. What a strong lady you are! Jean

I know that the upbeat attitude helped my healing, and I had no intention of being a victim. But I question how honest I was being with myself and whether or not I was just trying to be strong for ego or appearances' sake. I was certainly doing a good job of giving off the impression I was strong!

I was still, however, taking my recovery slowly and really trying hard to go day by day. I was eager to return to the world, and felt that after looking within, my next step was to see what that felt like in the outside world. But I hadn't even thought about a potential date to return to work. Often the pain in my legs was so bad, it was impossible to think about driving or doing much of anything.

I'd feel good, and then get knocked down. I guess it was that "nudge versus slap" thing again. The universe kept trying to tell me something and I was only half listening. I still had much to learn.

Tuesday, April 27, 2010

Re: Measuring Time When You Have So Much of It

Hello, all!

Yesterday morning I struggled to get up, having had a somewhat painful night (some are worse than others), and so I dozed on and off. I woke up to a knocking at my front door and, still in a daze, decided to ignore whoever was there. The knocking was persistent, though, so I looked at the clock and saw that it was 9 a.m. (My apologies to those of you who never get to stay in bed that late!) I then went into a panic — Oh, no! The nurse who comes to do my weekly blood work was here, and here I am lounging in bed like a slug, not ready for her!

And so I threw on a robe and without my brace (a big no-no), went to the front door, ready to grovel with apologies. When I got there, no one was at the door — except for this bird which then flew away! Remember the bird I mentioned that keeps pecking at my solarium windows? Same bird. I guess he decided it was time for me to get up.

And then I realized that it was Monday — and the nurse comes on Wednesdays. I am *really* going to get that bird.

When each day presents itself the same way, it's difficult to keep track of the days. My time right now is unmeasured, only punctuated by medicine doses. I don't need the clock for this; my body tells me when the next dose is due. The weather guy on TV usually gives me a clue as to what day it is, but I mostly forget. I am so unused to following a schedule that when I have appointments, I get a little worked up to make sure I remember.

And so, since I had a couple of appointments yesterday afternoon and didn't want to be late, I put my watch on for the first time since March 11th. I expected to struggle with the strap a little since it had been so long, but no, the watch went on easily. It's amazing how quickly and easily we can slip into our old skin and old habits. I did not, however, look at the watch until I was between appointments and trying to figure out if I had time to run an errand before the next one. The watch was an hour behind and said the date was the 22nd! Even though just that morning I'd been confused about the days, I knew that wasn't right. So all along, the watch wasn't measuring time for me. I was. Once again, I was living by segmented pieces of time, measured by how much activity I could do in that segment. I liked it better when I didn't know what day and time it was.

The watch is now back in my jewelry drawer, and it's still an hour behind. And although I haven't checked, I would guess that it now says the 23rd. After all, no matter where you're starting from, time does keep going.

My first appointment yesterday was a haircut, which was way overdue. Although that may not sound important, never underestimate the healing power in getting pampered a little and feeling like you look good! I'm thinking insurance should cover spa days.

The major appointment yesterday was with Dr. Dieckhaus in Infectious Disease. He wants to continue my IV treatment for another couple weeks, which was not a surprise since he had originally predicted six weeks. What was a surprise is that it will be followed by a minimum of six months of oral antibiotics. He said my blood work is looking good. The main piece they look at is the SED rate, which is an indicator of the amount of inflammation in the body. Although my number is still above normal, it has gone down drastically (from 118 to 28). The tricky part, though, is since I'm a walking billboard for arthritis, how will they know what's normal for me? Just like my crooked back, what's straight or normal for me is not what's normal for most others. I will need to find my own normal.

The doctor said it may mean that they decide to treat for a longer period with the oral antibiotics. He said that, in other cases, they would have done another surgery to remove all metal, cleared the infection and then, after the full course of treatment, re-do the surgery to put the metal back in. Yes, that's right, the surgery that gave me the infection to begin with! Well, before my blood pressure went up too high, he assured me that was not in the plan for me. One of the things I like about this doctor so far is that he doesn't appear to treat his patients as though they should all follow the same course. He understands the concept that what is right for one person may be way off for another.

And so today, nothing much has changed. I still did my IV this morning — although I have begun to notice how routine this is becoming. It's amazing to think that giving myself an IV twice each day would have ever gotten routine. But here again, I am aware of the drastically varying degrees of normal. I guess you can get used to anything if you have to. Sometimes, I long for normalcy when my days aren't filled with nurses, braces, medicines and couriers delivering medical supplies — and I'm lucky; I know those days are coming.

But it will still be different, because I am different. I'm still figuring out just what that means, but I believe that we are changed just by everyday life. Can't remember who, but someone once said, "You can't step into the same river twice." A former teacher of mine used to tell me that he believed you couldn't step into the same river once — that by the very thought and intent of stepping into the river, you have already changed it.

And although I know I will have schedules and appointments again, I hope I don't go back to living by the watch, measuring time. If you measure the time in your day and parcel it out into little segments of activity, how can you possibly be just where you are? You'll always be looking for that next segment of activity.

And just to prove my point — I didn't schedule a nap for today, but I just might take one!

As always, my thanks for your support and prayers!
June

———

At this time, I started noticing things more and became more introspective about the whole process — and I think I really began being more honest about what I was feeling. I didn't feel the need to impress anyone anymore with how strong I was being. Or maybe I didn't feel the need to convince myself anymore. With the medical side becoming more of a routine for me, I really began to turn inward and that's when the real journey of healing began. I had accepted my new norm or reality and finally had a little energy to begin the work I needed to do. I know I couldn't have done this if I didn't feel so completely supported. Being able to share my story was incredibly validating and uplifting. The kind words that came back to me continued to be touching and moving, and they demonstrated the power of universal love and connection. They showed me that, no matter what each of us endures, we are never alone. Help is just a thought away. I am inspired by the responses I received.

It sounds like things are very challenging, but you are definitely one to seize the moment, or hold it gently. I, too, have been on a path for spiritual transformation. I wish I could just hang out with you and share all kinds of stuff (between naps). Lots of love, Leslie

I'm happy to see that things appear to be moving in the right direction . . . finally?? Stay as strong as you are. You will come out on the other side a changed person. Patty P

Truly you are learning a lot through all of this, and I can't imagine it can be too easy. But your attitude and spirit are awesome!! Yes, I am finding it hard to just be, and instead feel like I'm going from task to task in my life! Know you are an inspiration! Laurie

You sound like you continue to manage with as much grace and ease as is possible. Thank you for sharing your story. One moment, one breath at a time. You'll get there! Love and blessings, Cheryl

Even when we think we "get it," sometimes life has new lessons in humility for us. The bird is most definitely bringing you a message. I suspect you are moving from annoyance with its pecking toward an openness to its message. God bless you, friend. I feel honored that you are sharing your journey with me. Liz B

We will have to give you some wine and lighten you up!!! That'll definitely have you losing track of time! Sue

---

I was especially inspired by Sue's response! It might help with that bird!

Wednesday, May 5, 2010

Liz was right. Even though I thought I was "getting it," life had more in store for me.

Re: More Changes

Hello, all!

I've spoken with some of you directly about this news, since it directly affected you. But for the rest of the group . . . a big change occurred this week.

I had my appointment with my spine doctor on Monday, and like the Type-A person I am, came armed with my list of questions — the most important of which was, "When can I go back to training?!!!"

I have been feeling like a slug, not contributing, worried about finances, old beliefs about having an obligation to work — I know these are not what I should be feeling right now and I need to let them go, but they were real feelings, nonetheless. My job right now is to heal, everyone tells me. But I have still been hearing those old tapes telling me I need to contribute, to work, to be significant.

And sometimes, when you refuse to let go of old beliefs and old habits, the universe has a way of forcing you to.

You can guess what my doctor's answer was. His very strong recommendation was that I do not return to work as a trainer — not now, not soon, and preferably not ever. My X-rays looked good, the fusion was intact, and everything was progressing nicely. But he felt that the degeneration he saw when he tried to repair my back was so significant that doing such a physically demanding job would put me at great risk. Although this is very hard for me to accept — not only did I really love what I did, but it's a big part of my identity — he told me in such a way that left me feeling like all was not lost. He said my meditation CD (he had gotten a copy just before my surgery) was one of the most beautiful things he had ever heard. He felt I should use my talents that way to help people feel better and focus on their spirituality. (Yes! A Western doctor talked about meditation and spirituality as being important!)

Well, I talked to Peter about it. And still refusing to let go, I told him that although this was the doctor's recommendation, in the end, it was still our decision as to whether or not I returned to work. And if we needed me to return for financial reasons, then I would do it. After all, I'm not Type-A for nothing! Peter's response was much like my doctor's. He felt that if going back to training could mean I might be severely disabled 10 years sooner than expected, then it wasn't worth the risk or the money. He also felt I could focus my energies on my CD (even though meditation is definitely not his thing, he has been very supportive). He said that, if I was honest with myself, I've really known this all along, that I've been in denial and it's about time I came out of it!

Those of us who do meditation, yoga, Reiki and other practices to try to create a more spiritual life use gentle words like letting go, acceptance, surrender. My husband? He just tells me to get out of denial, damn it, and get on with my life!

And so, I sit here with much of my "identity" gone, a blank page waiting for the rest of the story to come. I am no longer a trainer, and I'm getting to be okay with it. There are so many questions now: How do I make a living? What does that mean to my business? I even started thinking that I'll need to change my web page, my brochures, maybe even my logo and company name. (Watch out! Type-A steamrolling forward!) And once I stopped that track, I realized there's really only one question I need to answer: What does this mean to me? And in some ways, it's easier. Without the pressure to return to work, I really can focus on healing. It's getting easier to let go and surrender, and — yes, damn it — get on with my life! The path is right in front of me; I just need to step onto it.

And probably not surprisingly, the bird that was pecking at my windows is gone. He just disappeared. A friend of mine had told me to get an owl statue. Because owls are predators, it would scare the bird away. Well, I got an owl, but it's still in the house. I never got around to putting it out, and the bird is gone. I guess he didn't need to get my attention anymore.

I always thought I was a quick learner and a good listener, but it took many of you, my doctor, my husband and that bird (not to mention three surgeries and a life-threatening infection) to get me to see the truth and to feel like I could finally let go of old "stuff" and move forward. And if I'm giving you the impression that this is easy and I'm not scared, uncertain, floundering and resistant, I need a rewrite. In many ways, this is just as scary as the surgery was.

This was a big change for me — after all, I never thought I'd associate myself with the word "disabled." And I'm pretty certain there are many more changes to come. I've been feeling good physically and my back is healing well, but as much as that has been and still is a tough journey, I'm beginning to think the journey has just begun. Stick around. It should be interesting, not to mention entertaining!

With love and thanks for your continued support,
June

It was hard to let go of being a trainer; the work gave me great satisfaction and validation — and I really enjoyed it. But I also knew I was stepping onto new ground — learning to live outside of ego. For the first time in my life, I had to figure out how to just be me, without my accomplishments, goals and battles. I had never really known who I was today, since I had always been focused on what I had done yesterday and what I was going to do tomorrow. It was always about *doing*, not about *being*. Well, I was certainly going to have to learn the hard way. On some level, I realized having this opportunity was a great gift. But I admit I was truly scared about this part of my journey.

Thankfully, my friends sent their love and support and I knew I could step forward. They knew exactly what to say, and I was humbled by the depth of their feeling. I can always rely on their honesty — even when I don't want to hear it!

> *Things might seem uncertain now, but with your enormous energy and intelligence, I'm sure this so-called setback is just a new stepping stone. There is so much you can do! Frank*

> *Everything in time. Take the time to mourn the loss of this phase of your life and this one part of you. Then you can focus on all the other many parts of you. It's hard to admit to physical limitations, but your heart and mind are so much more than your body ever could be. I feel truly blessed that you are sharing your journey. You are helping people in ways you could not imagine. Continue to channel your energies to your healing process. Love, Carolyn*

Luv ya, June! Sounds like you are moving into an exciting new phase! Best wishes. Shaunn

As you know, one leg of the journey ends ... another begins! May you delight in the unfolding! Cheryl

Sounds like you are handling it all with grace. Continue on the path in that spirit, and you will understand and appreciate where it is leading you! Michelle

Bravo! I guess it took a village to get you to finally listen ... to what you really knew all along. This will be a great blessing in so many ways! Namaste. Richard

Congratulations, June! Letting go is one of the hardest, if not THE hardest things a human can do. You are re-creating yourself, but your identity is not gone at all. Just one of the hats you wore. Time to change hats! What's under that hat, what is wearing that hat, is still there. Your soul, your essence and your gifts, just waiting for you to take the next step. Walk your talk! Step back, breathe ... and spend some time with the real June! Dory

What an incredible feeling to know I was not alone! My life was about to change and, yes, I was scared. But I felt like I had a hundred gentle hands resting on my shoulders, sending me love, supporting me just for being me!

One friend sent me a poem she had written, called "Surrender." I'd like to share it with you here.

Surrender
By Kim Townsend

She came to me unexpectedly
And whispered in a sweet-sounding voice,
"I will be with you silently
'Till you send me away by your own choice."

Surrender

I questioned as to why she came,
Pondered how it is her I would need.
And would my life ever be the same.
Perhaps she came to plant a seed.

Surrender

My life had been going along
With the usual bumps in the road,
Always feeling I had to be strong,
Carrying my heavy load.

Surrender

The past is now simply history,
A path of wisdom attained.
The pain is a distant memory,
The self I have regained.

Surrender

Angel of Surrender, tell me please,
What I must let go!
My heart, my soul or anxieties.
Help me let my spirit flow.

Surrender

I had a dream that week. I was supposed to play the
piano for some performance. (Yes, I do play. It's not that
joke about the guy who asks the doctor if he can play the
violin.) It was a jazz piece. I hate playing jazz, but I was
prepared to do it anyway. In the dream, I had to find a
musician to accompany me. I went to my parents to ask my
father, who was a great musician. When I started talking to
my mother, we began to fight about a completely unrelated
subject. She was angry about something, although I can't
remember what that something was. She just screamed at
me and then walked away in a huff. My dad, who actually
passed away several years ago, sat there smiling during
our whole fight and then calmly asked me what I needed
for the performance. I told him I was thinking sax or

clarinet — two instruments he didn't normally play; his instrument was the trumpet. He gently took me by the hand. I stood up and we started walking.

And he said to me, not to worry. "I will accompany you."

We are never, ever alone.

Monday, May 10, 2010

7:42 p.m.

Re: All Things are Relative

Hello, all!
After six weeks of IV antibiotics, I was finally transferred to oral antibiotics, which I will be on for the next six months, minimally.

After the first dose on Sunday, I threw up. And although I had had nothing to eat, I continued to throw up for more than an hour. You can imagine what was going through my mind and how scared I was. You can take a medicine that has bad side effects for a week or 10 days, but for six months? Was I going to be sick twice a day for six months?

But I decided to take the next dose that night and keep it separate by at least an hour from any other medication. I gagged just thinking about taking it, but I knew that since I had thrown up the medicine that morning, that meant I wasn't getting the antibiotics I needed. I was more scared about the infection than I was about throwing up again.

Thankfully, I kept that dose down, and kept this morning's down as well. So since this is day two on orals, I can probably say I am on the road to recovery! I have a doctor's appointment on Thursday and, providing I am still well, the IV/PICC line will come out.

I'm telling you about the reactions because it's become clear to me that the path to recovery is not without setbacks. Every time I think I'm doing well, something seems to take me back a step — much like I said before — a dance of one step forward and another back. But you know, that's just life. As I told a friend of mine recently, life is a string of events — sometimes good ones, sometimes bad, sometimes mixed. We just seem to notice the bad strings more. And, okay, I'm in a bad string. But it will turn around, because that's what life does. And it is also true that you cannot enjoy the highs if you do not experience the lows. All things are relative.

My pain level is still pretty high — and sometimes I'm not very good at controlling it. But I want to tell you about my dog. His name is Buddy and he is a golden retriever. He is 11½ years old, has malignant melanoma, chronic Lyme disease and arthritis from ACL repairs on both back legs. He has trouble getting up and down stairs, but he still makes the effort. He hurts to chase the Frisbee, but he still enjoys the playtime. He gets excited when we come in and out and always comes to greet us. He puts his pain aside. Today, I noticed him looking at me and I knew that he was in pain. But he didn't whimper.

He didn't ask for attention. He holds his pain as simply a part of living. He experiences both the highs and the lows. To him, too, all things are relative.

That doesn't mean we should be stoic and not ask for help. And it doesn't mean it doesn't hurt. It does. It REALLY does. But it is a lesson to me every day to try to not let the pain keep me from doing the things that bring me joy. And if pain is a part of my every day, then so be it. I can choose to be a victim or I can choose to participate in life. Guess which one I'm choosing.

Every day, I pass through my family room. And the wheelchair they sent me when I left the hospital is sitting there. I should send it back. But it is a reminder of the time 10 years ago (I was 40) when my previous doctor said that if I didn't have the original surgery to fuse my back, I would be in a wheelchair by 50. Now I am 50 (okay, almost 51), and have had more surgeries than I ever thought. I've spent more time in that chair than I would ever want to. And I could easily be in it for the rest of my life, like my doctor predicted.

But just like my dog, I can choose to let my pain define me. Or . . . I can chase the Frisbee.

I so badly want to catch that Frisbee!

Love,

June

I was beginning to settle back and just look around, finally seeing what was before me. I had, at least for the moment, put aside thoughts of "what was to become of me" and just focused on getting through each day. With the knowledge that I was so completely supported, I could begin to feel what it was like to surrender — not out of necessity because of being so dependent and sick, but because there was nothing to fight. The battle I thought I was in just seemed to disperse into the air. I wasn't fighting, I was living.

And the responses I received seemed to concur.

> *You are on a huge transformational journey that is touching all aspects of your life. You are in the rock tumbler big time! I don't know where the universe will spit you out, but you are showing up for your process and are living it with so much consciousness and courage. Be well and ride the wave. Big hug! Doris*

> *I could never throw a Frisbee! Hey, if I work on throwing it, will you work on catching it? ☺ Gwen*

> *Throwing up is NOT FUN! I hope this week is a better one for you! Eileen H*

> *Love you! And love hearing from you! XXX Renee*

> *Blessings to you, June. Here, I'm tossing you a virtual Frisbee! You Got It!!!! Dory*

Dear June, I am holding you in my awareness as you move through this space and time. Resistance to "what is" creates tension. May you remember that acceptance of "what is" is just for now. The more compassion you can give yourself, the more you will contribute to your healing. If you need to use the wheelchair, it's just for now. It doesn't mean that you've resigned to it. Peace and blessings, Cheryl

Yes, I learned that Surrender does not mean Resignation.

Tuesday, May 11, 2010

It's about two months after my surgeries, and I realize my friend and teacher was right — my life would be different and I didn't have a frame of reference at the time to see what it would look like. I guess I still don't have that frame of reference because I still can't see it. Recently I discovered this quote from Pema Chodron, an inspirational Buddhist monk: "When inspiration has become hidden, when we feel ready to give up, this is the time when healing can be found in the tenderness of pain itself." Maybe the pain could tell me something.

When I found out I couldn't be a trainer anymore, one of my friends told me there were lots of different ways to help people. It didn't really matter what I did, as long as I did it with love.

There is a woman who works at the deli counter at one of the local grocery stores. She's been there a long time. At one point, I noticed she always seems to enjoy herself. When you watch her, it's so apparent that she's happy with what she does. She smiles, she remembers people's names, she's obviously enjoying her time, not just slicing meat. When I go there, she sometimes helps me to change my day — just by being herself.

I still wonder what I'll do for a job next, but this woman shows me the importance of living simply with heartfelt love and service. I have to get rid of old beliefs about what I should do and how I should serve before I can see a different way. In the meantime, I'm trying to be who I am, not what I do.

Okay, Pema, if I've got to feel the pain anyway, let me find the tenderness and the healing.

Monday, May 17, 2010

I still struggle with finding value in myself for "just being me" and feel unworthy of all the love and support that has been extended to me. I know this will be an up-and-down process; and I try hard to just go with it and not look too far ahead, walking more gently through this world with a greater kindness. From a medical standpoint, I still have much healing to do. But I'm discovering this journey is also about emotional and spiritual healing, and the physical part was just the vehicle in which it's being delivered. I know I'm not alone in feeling as though I am nothing without a job. But I also know this is a painful lesson I need to learn. I spent so much of my life defining myself by what I was doing — and I couldn't even be happy with that. I had to always look at what I was going to do next. What I did today wasn't enough.

If I can find a way to finally be comfortable "being," I will also find peace. But the process is slow. Or maybe I'm not as quick a learner as I thought I was.

7:42 p.m.

Re: I am adrift

Hello, all!

First of all — thank you for your continued support and patience in listening to me. I feel somewhat selfish continuing to share my story, especially when I know all of you are dealing with issues, too. Please know I am here to listen as well, and I am ever so grateful for your presence. I hope to be someone who supports all of you as much as you support me.

Lots has happened this week. Most prominently, my IV/PICC line was removed. Even though it was something a nurse could do, my doctor insisted on taking it out himself. And a procedure that actually lasted five minutes was a half hour of his time with me. He's an incredible doctor who actually has compassion and caring for his patient — imagine that!

Anyway, the line came out and I was amazed at how small the tube was (after all, it was in my vein and it hurt like hell going in), and I was also amazed at how much it bled. But by the time I got home, there was nothing much left to it, just a pin-prick hole. Something so intense was really not much of anything at all. How quickly a horrible experience can be just a distant memory with no real visual wounds.

On the bad side, my X-rays showed a problem in my right knee (my good knee) — my doctor believes it is CPDD (Calcium Pyrophosphate Deposition Disease). Basically,

I'm laying down excess calcium in not-so-good places. It's a side effect of this type of surgery, and the fact that I've had high blood calcium levels twice in the last year. I'll need to go back to my knee doctor for confirmation, but there's not much they can do for it right now anyway, since typical treatments would interfere with the fusion. So, I have to deal with the pain for now.

I have now been on the oral antibiotics a week and, although I spend five out of seven days a week sipping ginger ale for the nausea, it's not so bad. I have to tell you, my husband (Peter) has been great. While one day is okay, the next I may feel sick — and he rolls with it and helps me either way. He doesn't coddle me, but he steps in when I need it. I know he has taken on so much of the burden of our life with this, but he never complains or lets me worry. He understands when I hurt so bad that any touch is unbearable, and knows when I need to be held and hugged. I couldn't ask for anything more.

In the presence of so much love and caring from him and all of you, I am finding myself somewhat adrift. I don't know yet what is next; and, although I am trying to be patient, there is so much of me that wants to give back . . . yet, I don't know how. I could never repay the support I have gotten from all of you. And I don't know yet where my place in life will be.

And on the good side: I have been seeing these commercials for Nestle's with Rascal Flatts — never heard of them before I saw the commercials — where they have a campfire and s'mores. I told Peter about how having campfires, steamers, corn and s'mores were a big part of my childhood and how the commercials made me want to do that! So what did he do? He built a firepit in our yard so that we could do just that! We haven't had the pleasure yet, since I was not up to par this weekend, but we will soon. If you want to join us — you are all welcome! I can't do much else these days, but I can give you all chocolate!!!

I have also been fortunate in the last week that I've been able to spend some time with friends/former clients — and I am struck by how special those relationships were and continue to be for me. It makes a difference in my every day, which is full of time and speculation.

I know that life is all about the people you build relationships with. I'm slowly learning that it has nothing to do with your job. And I am thankful for that, since I don't have that to offer right now. As a close friend and teacher once told me, people will be with you because of who you are, not because of what you do.

I am so blessed. Thank you, all.

Love,

June

What would I have done without this incredible network of friends?! In the middle of this horrible experience, I am struck by the people I know who give so readily of themselves. Each day, I get dozens of emails, reminding me they are all out there for me, ready to share their love, their energy, their faith. We are not individuals in this world. We are all connected and share a single source of power. And I have never been more grateful for that than I am now. Perhaps that is the first lesson I have really learned through this. It takes a lot more courage to be vulnerable before others and accept their help than it does to fight on your own.

Their words continue to warm the cockles of my heart. What exactly are cockles anyway? No matter, the warmth is definitely there.

> *You are a blessing for those of us who call you friend. Renee*

> *Sending you much love and support so that you can deepen your connection to patience and your being-ness! I love that you were inspired to do something really cool and nurturing! Love, Kimberly*

> *Firepit and chocolate sounds great! My life too has taken some twists and turns. You are definitely not alone in the "adrift" mode! Know that you are loved, and the things you are open to learning right now are invaluable. This too shall pass, as my mom used to always say! Love you, Laurie*

> *Sorry you didn't have a good weekend, but in spite of that, you always sound so encouraging. I always feel*

like I'm not alone when I hear from you, and I get uplifted by your message. Donna

Chocolate? I am there!!! Let me give you a thought... be a seaweed. Yes, keep your roots anchored to the ocean floor. And no matter what the currents bring, or what fish bump into you, simply move with the waves and don't fight the fish — whether in the form of pain (piranhas) or jellyfish (eeek!!) Gwen

Find a miracle in each day and enjoy the journey! Pat

Dearest June, can you hold the space for your Self and your healing now? That is all that needs to be done. Every blessing, Cheryl

Monday, May 24, 2010

7:39 p.m.

Re: I am learning to embrace the Princess in me!

Hello, all!

After my last email, many of you sent wonderful words of wisdom, guidance and encouragement — all of which were very much appreciated and taken in. One friend, in particular, used the imagery of seaweed, which is also adrift but remains rooted to the ocean floor. She encouraged me to let myself drift with the currents and the waves, but to remember my grounding, which will help me to face the dangers of the sea.

I would much rather have been a delicate flower, swaying in the breeze, with my roots held firmly in the earth — but okay, I can be seaweed!

Other friends encouraged me to continue to celebrate the process, to hold myself gently in this space and remove myself from the outcome — another much-needed reminder. I love your responses! They help me to gain new perspective and keep me going.

Some days the pain is bad, some days not so bad. I wish I could determine the pattern so I could make each day better, but I am at the mercy of my body. And I struggle against accepting that it has failed me or that any of this will be somewhat permanent. Okay, let me be seaweed . . .

Today I had to go to the grocery store. I have been promising Peter I would make lamb (sorry, my friends who are vegetarians). It's his favorite, and I felt the need to do something nice for him in return for all he's had to put up with. But when I was going through the store, I quickly began to realize that most of what I needed to get was heavier than what I should be lifting — yes, even a four-pound leg of lamb, or a package of chicken breasts. I needed help to get things into the basket and into the car, and then took one item at a time out of the car into the fridge or freezer in the garage, and left the rest for Peter to bring in when he gets home. I can't even do grocery shopping! Goodness, did I feel useless!

When I was done, my poor dog, Buddy, who was panting from the heat, needed some attention — and I really needed to rest. So we grabbed some tennis balls and headed to the pool. Since I can't get any sun (because of the antibiotics), I sat in the shade, covered with a towel, and threw the balls into the pool for him to fetch. I was feeling like an incredible slug. It's one thing to be a stay-at-home wife when you take care of kids or the home — but I couldn't do anything! Bon-bons and soap operas are not for me!

And then I realized I couldn't even reach the roasting pan, or bend to put the lamb in the oven! How was I going to cook that meal for him?

I wasn't brought up to be this way! It's not who I am!

And so I began to think about my upbringing. Yes, my dad was a military dad, so productivity and results were critical, and you fought for every inch you got. I learned how to battle.

But for me, he also wanted me to learn about dance and art and music, to appreciate the finer things. He called me "Princess." And I remembered that my maternal grandparents (who were closest to us) called me "La Dun" (the u sounds like the oo in book). It was a colloquial, affectionate term for "duchess" or "little princess."

For my whole life, it has been easy to embrace the warrior in me. That had been drilled in me really well, as many of you know. But where was the princess? What happened to her?

And so that you know I'm not entirely crazy, my family on my father's side does come from French royalty. (I know, a lot of you are saying that explains much!) When Peter and I went to France last year, I had hoped to find the ancestral castle. Unfortunately, when I got back and continued my research, I found that we had been within 30 miles of it. My father's family had been lords of the French Court (so I would have actually been Lady, not Princess — darn!). But during the early 1600s, the family lost the castle in local feuding. Shortly after that time, the king was offering French nobility money to colonize what was then New France and is now Quebec. According to family stories, my paternal grandfather and grandmother's families (who had been feuding families from the same town), both took the king up on his offer — and later combined!

Anyway, I digress. But only to show that there is some history to this "princess" thing, at least from my family's perspective. But my first husband used to call me princess. At one point, Peter also called me princess. (Wonder why he doesn't anymore . . . ?) And many of the male figures in my life — friends of my father's, male friends of mine, former boyfriends — a lot of them called me princess; none of whom knew anyone else had used that term. And it has always made me a bit uncomfortable. I certainly do not feel or look like a princess or anything that being a princess implies.

When Peter and I first started dating, I asked him why he called me princess and he said it was because I seemed fragile, that he feared I would break, that he felt he needed to take care of me. Okay, let's get real — how could someone 5'10", and 1XX lbs. (you're not getting that out of me) be fragile! But maybe he knew something I didn't at the time. I was too busy being the warrior, and I resented the idea that anyone would take care of me. Or the idea that I could break! But think about the difference. Unlike a warrior, a princess' value is not in what she does, but in who she is. As a warrior, I was all about what I did — not sure I even wanted to know who I was.

And so, sitting by the pool, now feeling like my entire purpose is nothing more than to learn how to be a gentle, kind, loving friend, mother, wife and self, I am learning to embrace the princess in me. I have nothing else physically to give. I cannot "do" anything. Right now, I have to be the princess.

I am asking all of you, my fellow princes and princesses, to put on your crowns and join me. We so easily learn how to battle; why is it we don't learn how to embrace our right to be regal? Our right to simply be, without attachment to activity or production? And to be loved and valued for that! Amazing!

Be royalty with me. I can show you the royal "wave"; I've got it down pretty well!

Love,

Princess June

With the weather getting warmer and the pain and sickness subsiding a little, I was beginning to think this "not doing" stuff wasn't so bad! At some point, even the fiercest warrior has to take a break. I had essentially given myself a cease-fire. Life can't possibly be about battling every day. That's too exhausting. And life is not supposed to be that hard! We are just so used to fighting that we gear up to do battle every time something happens — instead of staying fluid and bending to let the blows go by us.

But our upbringing doesn't always allow us to accept the royalty in us; mine certainly didn't. It's more socially acceptable to be a fighter. Intelligence, capability, productivity, dollars — these things are valued. But what about the simple smile that makes others feel better, or the ability to listen and give a hug or a word of encouragement when needed? You can't put a price on them or necessarily make a living at them, but they do have value.

I'm realizing this journey did not begin with this physical "calamity" (can't think of a more appropriate word for it). This situation has simply allowed me to see where my life has taken me and it will help me to figure out what's next. I'm realizing I've been searching so hard, working so hard. Now, I have to stop. I don't have a choice. And I'm trying to figure out all the pieces that make up me — to acknowledge and value both the warrior and the princess — because they are both me.

I'm not a slug! I'm a Princess! And a warrior . . . but right now, a Princess!

> *I have raised three children by myself (a true warrior). I'm proud of them and myself, but I've noticed that when Mother's Day comes around, they don't really do anything for me! I've realized that I've been sending the message that I am a "warrior" and not a "princess" who should be pampered! Well, no more! Princess Patty P*

> *It's so true that we identify ourselves by what we do. I know that I feel lost when I have no deadlines or*

work activity going on. I can't imagine how frustrated you must be, since you're used to being so active. Love, Eileen H

I have seen both the warrior and the princess in you at different times. By most of all, I have seen a friend. I hope you are enjoying your usefulness as a ball thrower for Buddy! Sandy

Okay, so perhaps you are now the Little Mermaid! Seaweed WITH a crown!! Gwen

I wish I had some words of wisdom for you, but I can only acknowledge that I'm sharing your journey. While your body is undergoing such an assault, your mind and spirit seem to be gaining strength in the fight. Many blessings on you as you take each day and go forward. Eileen F

Princess June, your stories always give me food for thought. These are tough lessons, and as some of the people would say down here in the hollers, "You are workin' that seaweed, girl!!" Actually, they'd say, "What's y'all talkin' bout with that seaweed? That don't make no sense!" Love and laughter, Leslie

Oh, thank God! This has been soooooooooo long in coming. Years and years, actually! The warrior part of you that has commanded your life needed to be put aside.

I am so glad you see this now. You ran from person to person trying to get some insight. It was your body that finally said, "Okay, sit down and listen!" You have been all about "fighting" something — anything — defending and muscling. The princess had been forgotten. It's not about the entitlement, but the deservability. I myself have been a princess for a very, very, very long time — there is no need to battle anything! YAY! Dory

I can always count on Dory to tell me like it is!

Tuesday, June 1, 2010

12:19 p.m.

Re: I'd like to order some fun with that pain, please!

Hello, all!

I don't want to bore you with my history, but indulge me a moment to explain how I got here. As some of you know, my last major fusion surgery before this one was almost 10 years ago. Like now, I was faced with the kind of pain that debilitates the soul, a pain that isn't touched by any kind of drug except one that will put you completely to sleep — and that only works for a couple of hours and you wake up yet again in pain, unable to take another dose for several more hours. I learned pretty quickly that pharmaceuticals were not the answer. Like now, many nights I prayed for sleep to come. I wished for one of those big Acme hammers in the cartoons, just so I could get knocked out.

Soon after that surgery, I happened to meet someone who told me about meditation and guided imagery. When I was a child, I used to play at escaping my body (what I now know to be transcendental meditation and even astral projection). I didn't know what I was doing then, but this person's stories about meditation rang a bell with that experience. And so, desperate to find a way to escape my body again, I began my interest and studies in meditation and energy therapy.

It worked. In fact, it worked so well that one of my teachers (and you'll know who you are) always used to tell me that I lived in my upper chakras! God forbid I should ground — then I would feel my body! I learned how to acknowledge and then let go of the pain, and I was good at it. I could fly! It was the landing that was hard. What I didn't do was accept my pain.

Knowing my teachers were right (but apparently not fully understanding), I began a quest to learn how to be IN my body. I worked really hard in physical therapy and even harder to become a personal trainer. I used my body well and reveled in being strong and fit. Most of my days were spent being utterly and completely physical. And it felt good to be able to help other people experiencing the same issues of pain and disability. But it was all about controlling and conquering my body, certainly not accepting or loving it. Pain and disability were things to overcome. Get strong and you will be free!

Yeah, sure. Well it worked as long as I could keep up the fight. Stop fighting — stop for a second — and the pain would come roaring back. Meditation gave me a respite from the pain, helped me to sleep and gave me the energy I needed to keep the fight going. But I began to notice how polarized I was. It was either/or. I felt as though I lived in two separate worlds — and honestly, I did! This wasn't the answer either. I had missed the lesson somehow. I was certainly in my body, but something still wasn't right. And of course, with that revelation, the pain became more and more intense. I couldn't keep up the fight.

And so, sometimes, when you refuse to see the path or give up your old beliefs, the universe has a way of tapping you on the shoulder to get your attention. I had many such taps over the last 10 years. When I ignored them, they became slaps. I still refused to give up the idea that I had to be strong and keep fighting. And when I still didn't get it, the slap became a knock-down punch — and here I am now.

What was I supposed to learn? To accept my pain and my body, not to fight it. Acknowledge, ACCEPT, let go. I was forgetting a step. And it is not a case of being in pain and learning to suck it up and live with it. That carries a different kind of emotion and, therefore, a different kind of result. We all have pain and we eagerly take something to ward it off, to get rid of it. After all, unless you're a masochist, it's not really a very pleasant experience. I'm not a believer in enduring pain for nothing. I don't like hurting, not at all. But what I have been trying — and it seems to be starting to help — is a process of actually taking the pain in, and spreading it throughout the body, which seems to diffuse or lessen it. That allows me to see it and react to it differently. Instead of the pain being a big, hard menacing block, it gets broken up and becomes air — much easier to handle and breathe out. Acknowledge, accept and let go.

And now, even though the pain can be incredible, I am beginning to settle in to my new body. I try not to dwell on it and I'm actually beginning to accept this as normal and find humor in every day. It's not about "when life hands you lemons, make lemonade." Forget that! (Could have said something else here, but this is G rated.) I'm not pasting a smile on when I want to scream! You can't ignore that the pain is real or pretend it's something else.

It's about acceptance — not giving up, not complacency, not staying a victim — *acceptance.* It's about not only being where you are at the moment, but being *who* you are at the moment — and choosing to find the blessings, the kindness and the fun in all of it.

And to prove my point, let me tell you a story. Some of you have already heard this one. Hopefully, you'll get another chuckle out of it!

First, let me tell you about my bone stimulator — it is a battery-operated energy pack about the size of a deck of cards with a long wire coming from it. The pack clips to my brace and the wire hangs down and splits into two prongs. Each day, I attach two electrodes on sticky pads to my lower back. Those electrodes each have wires that then attach to the two prongs. Well the design isn't so great because the prongs can come undone and the whole thing starts to beep. Reattaching the wires means getting undressed.

Okay, now here's the story.

I was in Macy's returning some items that I had bought just over six months ago, but never wore. I was at the register, and the sales person was pointing out that their policy was no refund after six months (I was just a couple days over the limit). I showed her my brace, told her I'd been in the hospital and couldn't return them earlier. She called for a manager and we waited.

After a couple of minutes, it became difficult for me to stand up, so I started moving around, resting against the counter, shifting my weight, generally getting fidgety. Well, of course, by the time the manager arrived, I had managed to loosen up the wires of the bone stimulator and I started beeping. As you can imagine, both the clerk and the manager looked at me with some concern — and I had to reassure them that I was not carrying a bomb. I showed them the bone stimulator and explained that I couldn't do anything about the beeping, since that would require dropping my pants! I'm not so sure they fully believed me, because I got that refund rather quickly after that! So there I stood at the register, beeping like a truck backing up, with the two of them awfully eager to have me go away.

I started walking out of the store — still beeping — and as I passed by people, they would look around with alarm, or if they realized it was coming from me, look at me with concern. (It's a good thing I didn't pass by any security people!) I just smiled, said hello and continued on my way, beeping like a truck.

It took absolutely everything I had not to turn around and walk backwards out of the store!

I think of it this way: There is a box on a high shelf in my closet. It has my vanity and ego in it. I think I'll leave it there. It's more fun without it!

Moral of the story? If you want to get a refund quickly, bring something that starts beeping mysteriously. No, seriously, that's not it. Let's try this: Once you accept, you can have fun with any situation!

I can't wait to have more fun!

Love,

June

I had no idea how prophetic this email was at the time, but it was the beginning of learning to accept my body for what it is and still love it — something I (like many women) have struggled with my whole life. Whether it was weight, hair, skin, measurements, I approached my body like I did the rest of my life. Something was always wrong. Something always had to be fixed. I could be better, do better, look better. And the end result? I was never happy in my body and being where I was at the moment. And it really was quite funny. Worry about my weight or a blemish on my face? Did you SEE the scar running down my back or notice the deformity?! I would never have anywhere near the perfect body, no matter how hard I worked or fought. So I figured I had two choices: either

I could learn to accept my body and love it, or I could be miserable about it for the rest of my life.

I'm all for not being miserable, so right now I choose to accept my body as is. I'm still working on the "loving it" part; but I'm making progress — and I can even have some fun with it. Besides, I figure I've paid my dues with this body, so in my next life, I ought to get a really good one!

Actually, there's some truth in that. Have you ever noticed that the really "beautiful" people are the ones who are simply comfortable in their own skin, like being beautiful for them is effortless? Acceptance is the key. Joy comes from that level of acceptance, and it shines out as beauty.

My friends — all wonderfully beautiful and special — shared my joy.

> *I loved your insight on working with pain and how your relationship to your body and pain has changed over time. A question worth asking is: What old trauma, memories, messages are connected to this pain. Some unwinding of tension or release of pain can follow. Love, Doris*

> *You are definitely a priceless princess . . . keep beeping! Peace, Deanna*

> *Riding the ebb and flow of sensation is not easy, as you know. Sometimes we do it with ease, other times not. XO, Cheryl*

Thanks for the humor! As you know, I have my pain too. Mine can be anywhere from head to toe, or even emotional. But pain is pain, and it hurts just the same. Donna

Wonderful, June! Yes, have fun! Keep going — you're doing terrific work . . . "New" body? Had to giggle. Sure seems like that, huh? But the body is not new at all. It's the body you've had since before birth. Meeting it fully and getting to know its challenges is quite a journey indeed! Dory

I did feel like I had a new body, even though Dory was right — it was the same body I'd had all along. (Once again, was I searching for something else, only to find myself right where I'd been all along?) I didn't know what it could do or what it could handle, how it would move. It was like starting over physically, even though I knew it was the same body.

Saturday, June 12, 2010

1:44 p.m.

Re: Time is Abundant

Hello, all!

Most of you probably don't know this, but my husband, Peter, has also been experiencing some back and neck issues lately. About five years ago, he had two partial discectomies, lumbar and cervical. Now there is further degeneration, and he will begin physical therapy next week. (The family that hurts together stays together?)

On the scale of back conditions, this is a hangnail. But, unfortunately, pain is not comparative. He hurts, and his pain is every bit as real as mine. I can appreciate and respect the kind of pain he is in, and how encompassing and debilitating it can be. I guess you could say I know a little something about it. But being Peter, relentless in the pursuit of fun, he has refused to give up softball.

So last night, after a softball game, he was tossing and turning, obviously unable to get comfortable and it woke me up. It was about 1 a.m. and he had to get up at 6 a.m. To help us out financially because of my lack of income, Peter has been taking on home construction jobs on the weekends, in addition to his daily corporate life. There are times when this makes me feel extremely guilty and I fight the urge to do whatever I need to do to get back to work full time, regardless of the repercussions. But mostly, I'm sorry about it and wish it wasn't so; but I know I am not to blame and I don't have the control to change my circumstances right now — probably a subject for another time.

Anyway, realizing his time to get some good sleep was now limited, I offered to get him some Aleve so he could get quick relief. He was more concerned about the fact that he had woken me up! I said to him, "Don't worry about me. I have time to get more sleep. You don't."

Well, he took the Aleve and he did get relief and fell asleep pretty quickly. I stayed awake and began thinking about that concept of limited time, and how that perception changes our approach to solving problems and managing our lives. When we're in pain, we want to take a pill so we will be out of pain quickly. After all, we don't have time to hurt. When we want to lose weight, we look for a quick fix. After all, we must be thin immediately. We don't have time to be fat anymore. Where did this perception that time is limited come from? There are the same 24 hours in each day, whether we fill them or not. And no matter how quickly we move through the day or how fast we fix things, we will never have more or less than 24 hours. There is no such thing as "time to spare" because it's always been the same amount of time, no matter what we do!

I didn't learn this easily. When my son was about two years old, he would — like any other child — occasionally resort to typical terrible-two behavior. When the storm was over, we would go through this process where we would sit down and I would ask him, "What makes Mommy angry?" Invariably, he would say, "Tantrums." When prompted what else, he would add on, "Fussing and whining." A third prompt in our script usually brought forward, "Disobeying." But one day, he instead said, "Wasting time."

Talk about out of the mouths of babes! I realized that each morning, in our hurry to get out of the house and on with the day, I constantly said to him, "Don't dawdle. We don't have time to waste." He was probably the only two-year-old who knew the word "dawdle." I must have looked like the rabbit in *Alice in Wonderland*! It's amazing that my son's personality, as it has unfolded since, is so much more laid back. I guess he learned from his mother what NOT to do.

Although it may have seemed that way, I wasn't behaving as though time was precious. I wasn't treating time like a precious commodity — I was treating it like a scarce commodity! In fact, back then, I treated everything as though it was scarce. And over my life, I have had to learn the grace of abundance the hard way — again, another subject, another time.

Now, I have this wonderful gift of time. In my life right now, time IS abundant, and yet, I still only have the same 24 hours. Amazing, isn't it!

Try this someday . . . just take five minutes. We can all find five minutes, right? And during those five minutes, do nothing. Don't close your eyes, don't take a short nap, don't meditate, don't read, don't watch TV, don't listen to music, don't talk on the phone . . . Do nothing. Look around you and just notice what happens to your thoughts. Most of us would get agitated and antsy pretty quickly. We would feel guilty about not filling that five minutes with something productive — or at least something, anything.

I used to be a lot like that, and the thought of a couple of hours with nothing to do stretching out ahead of me would send me into a panic. Now I have entire days unfilled — and no, I don't spend all of them just doing nothing. But I know I can take five minutes or whatever time I need. I've been given this incredible gift of understanding the abundance of time; and what's amazing is I still manage to get done whatever needs to get done. Most importantly, it is teaching me how to be still. Even though the clock keeps running, I'm learning how to stand still — and if I look hard enough, I know that in that stillness, I will find me.

So when my pain keeps me from sleeping or doing something, I can be patient, wait it out and not reach immediately for a pain killer. And you know what? The pain always subsides — and in the same amount of time it would take for a pill to work. When I am sick from the antibiotics (which is happening more and more often these days), I try not to fight the nausea and get worried about what needs to be done or fret about not wanting to be sick. I can just allow myself to lie down and be sick instead of fighting or pushing on. And you know what? The sickness always goes away — just as fast (probably faster) than if I had continued to fight it.

I know that it's not easy — many of you have businesses to run, jobs to go to, children and families to care for, civic obligations. There always seems to be too much on our plates (and we get frustrated and resent it, even though we're the ones who filled the plate).

But my point is that time is like any other resource in our lives. If we believe it to be scarce, we will live with that scarcity. If we believe and act as though time is abundant — giving ourselves the time and moments we need to process, heal, grow, play, connect, love and simply be still — we will always have more than enough time.

I was given a rare opportunity to be able to let go of most of my responsibilities and focus on myself. Although it has come with a painfully high price, it is a luxury and I know it. But I believe we can all still come to a place where time is abundant and we are not afraid to take the time to find stillness in the middle of our hectic lives.

Be still, my friends.

June

"No thought, no action, no movement, total
stillness: only thus can one manifest the true
nature and law of things from within and
unconsciously, and at last become one
with heaven and earth."
Lao Tzu

"Learning how to be still, to really be still
and let life happen — that stillness
becomes a radiance."
Morgan Freeman

"One's action ought to come out of an achieved
stillness: not to be mere rushing on."
D.H. Lawrence

The lesson of stillness resonated well within me, and
it is true — when you take the time to care for yourself
and find those moments of stillness, you will also find
all the time you need to be productive. Those days of
rushing around, trying to fill every moment, doing more
in five minutes than Superman could — those days are
well behind me. Amazingly, I still find myself busy, but it
doesn't have the same frenetic energy, the same desperation.

It was so tempting to push forward to recreate my
life, to put it all back together, create an identity, create a

living, put the details of my career together again. I knew how to do that. What I was learning was how to have the patience to let it all turn out the way it was supposed to, giving myself the time I needed to be still — because in that stillness, the answers would come.

It is hard to allow the universe to steer us as opposed to trying to inflict our will upon it. I'm with you on this. I'm getting better at it, but it is still constantly a challenge. Be well, George

Great work! Stillness brings great clarity of vision! Dory

I can take a deep breath and let go. It's getting easier.

Wednesday, June 16, 2010

10:03 a.m.

Re: I can't wait to get this ******* brace off! (Keeping it G rated, remember!)

Hello, all!

The brace definitely represents a love-hate relationship, a clear case of putting up with something awful that's supposed to be "for your own good."

Tomorrow, I have an appointment with my spine surgeon. It is, at least in my perspective, a momentous one. This is the three-month mark, and that is the average time for wearing the brace. We will take X-rays, and my doctor will look them over. Because he really is a nice guy who really cares about his patients, he will look at them very carefully before saying anything. And then he will patiently explain to me everything he sees. He will wrap the bad parts in words of encouragement, and he will try to focus on the good parts, giving me all the credit for simply sitting back and letting nature heal me. He will applaud me for being a good patient and assure me that we are on track and that the fusion is healing well. He will be sure to remind me the recovery process is long and it will take time.

During all that, I will probably be holding my breath, mentally screaming for him to get to the bottom line. Because what I'm really hoping for is that he will follow all that up with the words, "YOU DON'T HAVE TO WEAR YOUR BRACE ANYMORE!" I swear to God, at that point, I will either jump for joy (at which point he will admonish me — no impact movement), I will faint from relief or pee my pants from the excitement. Well, maybe not that, but you can imagine how happy I will be!

I have done okay with the brace these last 102 days (but who's counting?). I have dealt with wearing my husband's clothes — to say I look frumpy would be a compliment. I have ignored the pitying looks in public — and actually played it up sometimes to get some help! I have not gotten frustrated when I've felt clumsy and huge, and I have let my vanity take the beating. After all, if it will help me to heal, I'll do it.

Let me give you a few examples as to how this brace has been so endearing to me . . .

Putting it on in the morning is a major ordeal. If it's not really tight, it doesn't work. So each morning I pull it as tight as possible, like Mammy pulled Scarlett's corset tight — except that the result is a 38-inch waist of plastic brace, not an 18-inch one. When I'm done, I'm left splayed on the bed, unable to move. I must look like I'm nine months pregnant when I try to roll to get up! Talk about beached whales . . .

And no matter how tightly I pull the straps, the brace always loosens up during the day, which means it rides up. By the end of some days, I feel like Oscar stuck in his garbage can, with only my arms and head sticking out.

When I take the brace off at night (especially on warm days), my T-shirt is stuck to my body and I have to peel it off me. It's like taking off a layer of skin. And I hate to say it, but it seems no amount of deodorant, perfume, open windows or Febreze will clear the air. But Peter never complains. Love must not only be blind, but it must also have a stuffy nose!

I have permanent bruises on my hips where the brace presses in against the bone. And, I fear, another permanent bruise on my knee where I keep hitting the bedpost after bouncing off the dresser because I can't seem to remember how big I am in the brace! Getting to the bed is like maneuvering through a pinball machine.

One day I was in the bathroom brushing my teeth. The door was open right behind me. I took a step back and didn't watch what I was doing. I got the back bottom edge of my brace caught on the doorknob and got stuck there, like a scarecrow on a pole. When I tried to dislodge myself, I stepped forward and, of course, the door came with me — and clunked me on the back of the head.

Another time, I was out to lunch with a friend. We were seated at a booth. When I went to sit down on the soft cushion, the brace slid up — and when it did, it made a sound. One that I'm sure you all know. Very ladylike!

It has been SO much fun!!! But, I'd like to put this toy away now, thank you! Unfortunately, the brace is a critical (and challenging) part of the recovery process, and there is no way to go through it except for with tolerance, patience and humor. Hence, the challenging part . . .

More importantly than just freeing my body from the brace is the milestone in my recovery that this will mean. It's a marker that all really is going according to projections. And it means I get to begin the next phase — physical therapy, which, though it will be intense and painful, will also be a great step. Not only will there be lots more toys to play with, but I get to be active in my recovery, which will help to give me a sense of moving forward.

And so, one more time, I ask for your prayers and well wishes! Think of me on Thursday with the hopes that the fusion is healing and I will finally be able to retire my most favored and stunningly sexy accessory!

As always, I am so very grateful for your support, guidance and caring. Someday, when I can look back on all of this, I will be able to smile because I did not have to do it alone. For this, I am incredibly blessed.

Namaste,

June

Finding the humor in the brace made it much easier to handle. After all, what sense did it make to get all upset about a hunk of plastic? I refused to expend energy on something I just had to live through, but I really was ready to get rid of it! One friend suggested it would make a great show-and-tell. I would, of course, have to resist the urge to therapeutically smash it into itty-bitty pieces.

Actually, as horrible as the brace was, it, too — like my friends — was instrumental in "supporting" me through this time. It was a great daily reminder that I was supported both physically and emotionally and, with that support, I could deal with the many lessons I found myself now faced with.

> Wow! What a journey toward recovery! Good luck Thursday and every day. Carmen H

> Best of luck at the doctor visit. To say you have great patience would certainly be an understatement! Jean

> I can actually see and hear you telling these stories of the brace – you are a riot! I hope all goes well Thursday with the doctor, and I will certainly be holding you in thought and healing prayer. And if you keep the brace, as a "stunningly sexy accessory", perhaps you can use it for those "special evenings"!!! Too funny! Keep laughing. Life is outrageous! Dory

Friday, June 18, 2010

8:08 a.m. (An early morning for me!)

Re: I am freeeee!!!!!

Hello, all!

My thanks to everyone for their warm wishes, thoughts and healing energy . . . it apparently worked, because my doctor was "ecstatic" about the way my back looks. So he released me from my plastic, somewhat-smelly prison and the turtle is now without her shell. He's a little superstitious, though, and asked me not to throw the brace away — that would just be inviting the need to use it again! So I must resist the urge to therapeutically smash it into a thousand pieces, and instead stick it in the closet, where it will be a continual reminder of my new-found freedom!!! And a reminder not to try to do too much — or do anything stupid — so I won't need it again!

I start physical therapy in a little over a week, and now it's just a matter of time to let the fusion heal and the muscles rebuild. The doctor did not see any potential complications — no loose screws . . . at least, not in my back — and he expects some if not all of the nerve pain in my legs to subside over the next year.

I feel a little wobbly and vulnerable, and I think I walk funny. The first thing I noticed, though, is that — compared to before the surgeries — it's easier to stand up straight. I know without the brace's support, I will probably tire more easily and hurt more until the muscles get strong enough to do their job again. A temporary step back in order to take a giant leap forward! I am encouraged because last night, after a half day without the brace, I did not hurt as much as I would have expected.

I am more than ready to begin this next phase, but will have to remind myself to continue the healing process in a "kindler, gentler" way. This next part is when the real hard work begins; and that's something I do well (when the going gets tough . . .). I intend to approach the PT differently this time. I will still work hard, but I will also keep an awareness of my body and be kind to myself. With that awareness, I will notice each small step of improvement and not wait until a final outcome to celebrate my progress!

It's definitely a day for champagne! Cheers, everyone! With gratitude and love,
June

I felt like a race horse at the gate (although one friend asked me to remember a different race with a turtle and a bunny). I was so eager to move forward and run the race at full speed. Trying to listen to all the lessons I had learned about stillness and balance, but a little hard of hearing from the "celebration." But hearing the cheers from my friends was also important, and so I guess it was okay if I forgot to be still for a moment. A steady stream of encouragement came in to my in box: *Congratulations, Good Work, Yay, Great News, Hurray,* and even a *Yipeeeeeeeeeeeeeeeee!* My friends were not only happy for me, but I could also tell that they really FELT my joy. It made me feel even more blessed that I could share my story with them, and that they were so eager to hear it.

> *Congratulations! Enjoy that champagne; you've certainly earned it! Carrie*

> *Congratulations! You are such a strong person. Thank you for sharing! Eileen F*

> *Fantastic news! You made the journey to this point with true grace, embracing each day as an opportunity to practice, practice, practice (as a Zen master would say)! Michelle*

> *Celebrating with you! Cheryl*

> *Thank God, and good work, June! Shaunn*

Congratulations! I think you have a good approach in mind — slow, easy and aware wins the race. Remember the Tortoise and the Hare . . . Be well and enjoy your new freedom of movement. George

Go, girl, go!!!!! Doris

We are thrilled at the latest news. Our thoughts are with you. Paul & Eileen H

Yay for getting out of brace prison! Think of it as being on probation. As long as you don't have any violations, you won't get sent back! Love, Carolyn

Sunday, July 4, 2010

1:34 a.m. (Yes, a sleepless night.)

Re: The road to my recovery is apparently filled with potholes.
But what's a few bumps in the road?

Hello, all!
I fear this is going to be a longer one than usual since it's been a while . . . please bear with me and thank you for continuing to listen. I've started writing this email several times, and I'm not sure why I didn't send it out. Maybe I just don't want to send out any "bad" news and I'm sure you don't want to hear any more of it. But will you all believe me if I tell you that I'm really okay, in spite of recent events? It's not denial, or the fact that I'm beginning to feel sucker punched and a bit numb to it all. I'm really doing okay, on many levels.

As some of you know, a couple weeks ago I had a setback — minor in the scheme of things, but one that left me in a limbo that in some ways was worse than a major calamity with a definitive cure.

I developed hives. At first I thought it was just a minor reaction to the sun — even though I lather on SPF 50 before I leave the bedroom each morning and I am never in direct sunlight. (I'm auditioning for the next Twilight sequel soon.) But when the hives went down, I was left with red, scaly blotches — not a typical "photosensitivity dermatitis." And so, after the weekend, I called my Infectious Disease doctor's office (it is still amazing to me that I have an infectious-disease doctor!).

Anyway, my doctor was in Africa (he runs an incredible public-health service program there a couple of times a year) and his on-call doctor saw me. Long story short — everyone was concerned because the "rash" didn't look like anything typical and the first thing they did was take me off the antibiotics, since the medicine enhances photosensitivity and at any time another dose could put me into anaphylactic shock. (The good news is that the antibiotics were making me sick, so now I don't have to worry about that!) So the worst part of the whole episode was wondering if the infection would come roaring back while I was off antibiotics. The real big concern is that this bacteria has a nasty habit of attaching to the coating on the hardware that's holding my spine together. Without the antibiotics, if the bacteria spreads to the hardware, I am in serious trouble.

Options were to put me on a different antibiotic (but because of other allergies, I'm running short on those options) or back on the IV. And although I went through a couple weeks of uncertainty, once again, I lucked out. My regular doctor came back from Africa on Wednesday and insisted on seeing me Thursday morning (even though he wasn't scheduled to work). After extensive blood work by his colleague and a consultation with a dermatologist, the end diagnosis for now is a "severe" photosensitivity reaction compounded by the antibiotics. I am now on steroids and then will begin a new antibiotic on Wednesday. Megadoses of Keflex. Oh, boy. Another four to eight months to go.

But I have to tell you that, even with the uncertainty — which can be much more stressful than a definitive bad event — I really felt pretty good! In fact, I recently celebrated mutual birthdays with a good friend of mine and she told me I must be faking it because I looked great! I feel great. This latest episode is just one small blip. I am like Keanu Reeves in The Matrix, dodging bullets, just moving aside . . . feeling graceful, peaceful. It's all really getting rather boring. What was that I said earlier about the relativity of normalcy? That this kind of stuff can seem normal after a while?

Not to make a major shift, but — my son was in a car accident this week. Yes, he is okay. But he found out he was dealing with an uninsured motorist who was trying to cheat him — so he's 25 and was suddenly faced with the evil of the world, the reality that some people will not take responsibility for their actions, not all people are trustworthy and that bad things can happen to good people. And it was hard on him. He's in Pennsylvania, not local, and so over the last few days, we've spent a lot of time on the phone. He told me that, in spite of everything, he didn't want to ruin this guy's family by filing a police report, which would take away the guy's license. He felt bad causing further harm to get his justice. But he knows he is faced with that decision. And part of him felt like he was being a wimp for not destroying this guy. His "rude awakening" has been more painful than anything I've experienced in these surgeries. Emotional pain, disappointment, the destruction of dreams — these are pains that last.

And the fact that he is agonizing over it tells me he is a good person. Action out of revenge is a no-win situation. I am proud of him. And I know his pain is real.

But during our talks, there was something he said to me that I thought was interesting. He said, "If the person you were 15 years ago met the person you are today, would she recognize you?"

As I've said in a previous email: Out of the mouths of babes . . . the answer is no. I am constantly amazed at his intuitive capabilities. I was a hyper Type-A person who didn't understand about acceptance and I wonder what his childhood would have been like if things were different, if I had been different. Before, it was all about winning a battle over life. Today, I was able to give him insights I never would have been able to ten years ago in this situation. I tried to talk to him about the idea that life (and its bad parts) are relative, that you're only a victim if you choose to be one. There is no dark without the light and vice versa. That life is not about whether or not bad things happen to you; it's about what you do with them.

And whether or not you can get through the end of the day making choices and expressing yourself with true integrity. Then you can go to sleep with a smile. There's no right or wrong, only what is truly you.

(At this point, he said, "Mom, you're not going to give me that new-age stuff, are you? I'm not going to meditate!")

And so, there are no coincidences in life . . . things happen for a reason . . . whatever phrase you'd like to use. There are so many lessons occurring. And yet, so many blessings happening in the middle of it all — and I know that seems hard to believe. There are lots of potholes, yes. As another friend said, "Will it never end?" No, it won't. And that's okay. It's just all part of life.

I don't believe that my circumstances are "bad" and I don't believe I'm being especially brave or strong as some people have said. My situation is just simply reality, no different from yours. And it flows from one day into the next, just like yours (except mine is probably a little more boring). It's not the situation that's bad; it's how I react to it. I choose not to be a victim.

The hard part is not the physical part, believe it or not. I have a great doctor, and a great physical therapist who has been with me for 10 years now. It's the transformation of my life that is the real work. It's the beginning of really, truly integrating both the physical and the emotional and spiritual. There's no blueprint for it. Lots of books and articles and seminars, but no one really has the secret, no matter what they claim. Trust me, I've tried them all. I've been through the physical stuff before, and I work on the spiritual side, too. But I haven't really been faced with this place of completely losing myself, losing the person I know to be me.

And although that is the hard part, it's also been the interesting part. Because, through it all, I'm finding out who I am, rediscovering who I was and who I have been — all along.

With much love, thanks and grace,

June (a.k.a. Bella — I'll be the one by the pool this weekend with a long-sleeve shirt on and covered with a towel. Bright light! Bright light!)

I felt somehow softer here, finished with the "celebration" and managing to hold back the reins on my racehorse ways. I had settled into a more peaceful and aware state, still approaching physical therapy with vigor and intensity, but listening to my body and responding in kind. And under that peaceful state there was still joy — a quiet smile, perhaps the beginning of self love. I didn't do that "intentionally." I wasn't trying to be or do anything in particular. It's just how I felt. Maybe some of the lessons were sticking this time.

And I can't say this enough: Knowing how loved and supported I am made it all possible.

Your spirits sound so much better. I know that it's hard, but you will pull through all this. It's just gonna take a little longer . . . a few years from now you will be able to look back on your struggles, and they will then be a thing of the past. Dee

It's always nice when we discover — sometimes over and over again — that we're inside there someplace. Shaking off the scales and letting the universe drive sometimes is helpful, but I know from experience that it can be hard to do. Continued good luck and keep the faith. George

Holding you in my awareness and grateful to witness your blossoming during these challenging times. Glad to hear you and your son are out of harm's way. Love and peace, Cheryl

Monday, July 12, 2010

10:51 a.m.

Re: My pain is talking, and I'm listening!

Hello, all!

I started physical therapy recently and, although I was eager to get started on the next phase of my recovery, I cautioned myself to listen to my body and take it slowly. The first session was an evaluation and a few exercises. Not bad. I did the exercises at home and felt good that there was no residual or increased pain. Feeling pretty good . . . listening to my body . . . nice and gentle . . . doing okay.

And then came the second session. Oh, my God! He kicked my butt! Those of you who were my clients, you can stop chuckling now. I know, what goes around comes around. I am a marshmallow compared to him. By the end of the hour, my hair was dripping wet, as if I'd just come out of the shower. It was a long ride home.

But it felt really great to work hard again. There is a wonderful satisfaction that comes from the physical release, and I've missed it over these last few months. At the same time, I'm trying to keep an awareness of moving too far toward the physical and ignoring the mind/body connection. Luckily for me (or not so luckily), my body has a way of continuing to force me to pay attention and not do too much — it hurts like hell. Pain is the body's communication tool, and it's highly effective.

A friend of mine asked me recently if I was still in pain. I had to stop for a moment to think about it and check in, because it's no longer something that sits at the front of my mind, constantly pressing for my attention. I decided that, yes, I still hurt, but it's not a 10 anymore. On a regular basis, I'll have zaps in my legs from the nerve endings firing, sharp pain in my hips and incredible achiness in my mid back. I have trouble sitting, standing, and I still walk funny. But it's really a matter of saying "ouch" and moving on. I acknowledge the pain, accept that it's there, decide if it means making any changes (posture, activity, etc.) and then let it go.

I don't try to control my pain, push it away or mask it. The more you try to control pain, the bigger it gets. If you try to block out the pink elephant in the room, it just gets bigger and becomes a brighter shade of pink. When your pain keeps talking, you don't tell it to shut up. You have to listen to it — what is it trying to tell me? Breathe through it and decide if it will change your choices. Then make those changes, or not, and move on. Keep breathing.

Pain is not the enemy. It's a valuable tool that keeps you connected to your body and forces you to pay attention.

Pain, like life and stress, is not about handling, managing or getting control. It's about experiencing and living through it — working with it, not against it. Trust me, if you try to fight pain, you will lose.

Another friend was telling me about her back pain, and then she stopped. She felt like she couldn't "complain" to me about pain. But one thing I've learned is that pain is not comparable. If someone is in pain, it's real and it doesn't much matter what anyone else is experiencing. They have a right to experience their own pain, talk about it or do whatever they feel they need to do to get relief, even if it's just venting.

Besides, on any given day, I can most certainly find someone else who is worse off than me.

And so, at this moment, I am thinking of you all and hoping that the pain you may be experiencing in your life is somehow lessened today — if for no other reason than because someone else is willing to share its burden. I know that having all of you has worked miracles for me.

With blessings and love,

June

I was settling in and beginning to accept the fact that this pain was not going to go away — not with a pill, not with more surgery, not with physical therapy. I would get stronger, but moving — and not moving — would always be painful. It's my reality, at least for today. But that didn't mean I was about to give up and stop trying to get as mobile as possible. I was not afraid of my pain. It did not define me. But it was part of me and I had to accept it.

Some of my former clients loved to hear that my therapist had pushed me hard! And other friends told me stories of their own pain or the struggles of someone dear to them. I was honored that they shared their pain with me, since they had allowed me to share mine with them. I could share honestly and completely because I knew I would be supported and not judged. I didn't have to push anything away or leave anything out. And in that simple, honest sharing, I found real healing.

> *Pain is like meditation, isn't it? The more we try to block out pain or thoughts, the more they come in!!! Gwen*

> *How wonderful to enjoy such physicality! Blessings for your PT journey! Cheryl*

> *So good to hear from you, sweetie. You share so deeply — I love that about you. I'm glad you're turning away from being an Amazon. Life has a way of telling us when our best coping techniques need some tweaking. The work I've been doing has been physically and emotionally draining. Please keep me in your prayers. I think about you often, and your amazing journey, and how you are willing to scale the mountain and plumb the depths. Sending you hugs! XX Leslie*

Thursday, July 22, 2010

10:05 p.m.

Re: Where's the passion?

Hello, all!

A few nights ago, I had a dream. It was very strange. I dreamed that I was going back to college. I moved all my things in, and the living quarters were set up so it was really like living at home, with all my furniture, etc. The school campus was all connected, so all the "dorms" and main buildings were under the same roof. After moving in, I went looking for the class-registration area. I couldn't find it. I went through gyms and cafeterias and climbed up stairs and down stairs. There was a lot of activity in all the places I went through. And everyone kept giving me directions, but I kept struggling to find the right place.

I finally found an open area that looked like a gymnasium, and it was filled with tables marked with segments of the alphabet and lots of people talking. I went to the table marked with H for my last name. A young guy was at that table. He was very confident, somewhat arrogant. I told him I wanted to register for classes.

He leaned back on his chair, teetering back on its two legs. And he looked at me for what seemed like a full minute. He didn't invite me to sit in the chair in front of his table. All he said to me was this: "When you know what your passion is, you can come back and learn."

Some of the good part of living a more even, balanced life is that you are living a more even, balanced life. Some of the bad part is that you are living a more even, balanced life. What I'm having trouble getting used to is that it doesn't feel passionate. I feel like I'm losing a part of myself that is important. My passion, although it has sometimes been detrimental, is who I am. It has caused me great grief and pain. It has caused me great joy. And I need to find it again.

Not to change the subject — actually it's on subject . . . physical therapy has been grueling. Brian (a.k.a. the greatest therapist on earth and possibly the most sadistic) really works me hard. Although every week I feel stronger and see the difference, I recognize that I need more recovery time. A part of me has become increasingly aware that I am older. But I will not give up. I will not let this beat me. And if that sounds like the old "battle" person, I think in these circumstances I need to pull out the warrior in me. It is time.

But it's made me look at passion. Because the last time I went through this, it created a passion in me to work with others. And now, that's not possible. So I'm having trouble figuring out where to put that energy. It's not changing how I work at it — I've noticed I'm the only person who leaves that place drenched in sweat. But I'm still having trouble seeing the future. And my place in it.

I can work hard physically — and honestly, it feels good. Really good. I can work hard spiritually, and that feels just as good. But I can't seem to connect the two and figure out where I'm supposed to be.

Life is easier now, on so many levels, even though I'm still dealing with pain and hard work to get back to normal — whatever that means. But on another level, it's also getting harder. I am no longer certain about what's next. It's scary.

But what I do know is this: I need to find my passion again.

May you all be blessed with a life of passion. There is no greater life.

June

There was a real sadness here, and I don't think it was the loss of passion I was really mourning. I was still dealing with feeling like I had no value without doing. I was still wondering who I was and felt as though I had no future. And so, I latched on to "passion" because I just wanted to feel . . . something — anything. I wanted a purpose and a direction that would fire me up!

This was a truly dark and difficult time. Physically, I was improving; but emotionally I was a wreck. To be truthful, I was feeling a bit sorry for myself, in spite of my striving to have an "enlightened" viewpoint. I was perilously close to giving up. What's interesting is that due to some technological glitch, this email never got to my friends. A week or so later, I got email messages asking why I hadn't written lately, and letting me know they missed hearing from me and they had been moved and inspired by my words. I had intended not to write again, and I had actually written a final email which I never sent out.

Monday, August 6, 2010

Journal Entry — The Final Email that was Never Sent

Hello, all!

This is the final email I'll be sending out. I've bent your ears long enough and I thank you for being out there, listening to me.

It has been, and still is, an incredible process. I'm still dealing with allergic reactions to the antibiotics, side effects and, of course, physical therapy. PT is very hard. I am there almost two hours and leave wiped out. I work hard and I know I have no other choice. Well, we all have choices. But let's just say I don't much like my other choices. And so I work hard.

But in many ways, PT is the easy part of my life. The rest is figuring out where I fit it, how I fit in. PT is easy in comparison. It gives me purpose.

I will be in PT for several more months and on antibiotics another four to six months. But so far, everything looks good. My blood work looks good (which means no major damage so far to my kidneys or liver). And I'm progressing well, moving quickly along. All that's left is determining what the hell I will do with the rest of my life. No big deal, except when you don't see much of a future of providing value and meaning.

I guess when you surrender, you really surrender.

My life has become simple in many ways. Each day, I have no more to worry about than to just hope to be the best friend, mother and/or wife I can be. But who am I when I'm not being one of those?

I guess I had already forgotten how to be a Princess!!! And the little glimmer of self-love I'd seen earlier was definitely gone. Some lessons I apparently had to learn and relearn. I never sent this email out and hesitated still to send another one at all. I felt unworthy of the love and support I was getting. I couldn't value myself; how was I of any value to anyone else? I was retreating somewhat and dangerously close to severing myself from the one thing that had been instrumental in my healing — my connection to others.

I don't look at this period as a setback. It was merely part of the process. Each one of us goes through life reaching out and then pulling back in. We respond to life like breath — expanding and contracting. I didn't consciously know I was doing this, but I know now that to retreat was what I needed. Had I continued the outward expression at this time, I believe I would have put on a mask and my emails would have become false — and in the end, that would have hindered my process more than going within.

I was going inside to put some substance to the reality of my pain, to accept that it would always be there. But I also began to recognize this was not the type of pain that was an alarm signal (like the pain you feel that tells you to take your hand away from the fire). This pain wasn't telling me to stop what I was doing or that I was harming myself. Understanding this allowed me to relax a bit more with the pain — and stop fighting it.

Fortunately, my support network did not desert me. They continued to encourage me to write again to them. They were not only listening to my story; they really wanted to hear it. It took me a while, but I started up again a couple weeks later.

Tuesday, August 17, 2010

8:35 a.m.

Re: Being "Scarlett"

Hello, all!

I know it's been a while since I sent anything out. Sometimes the days are so much the same that I feel like I don't have much to say — which for me could be a first!!! But here's what's been going on in my world lately . . .

Yesterday, I went to my Infectious Disease doctor. Whenever I go there, it's a surreal experience. When you walk into the waiting room, you look around and know that everyone there is dealing with, that's right — an INFECTIOUS disease! There are posters for HIV and other horrible diseases on the walls and I've noticed people choose to sit far apart from each other. You almost expect the nurse to come out in a hazmat suit!

But they are quite nice there, probably in part because the vast majority of patients are really very sick. My situation is nothing in comparison, and I always send up a prayer of thanks for me and blessings for them.

But I have good news: Everything looks great! Because there is really no way to know if I'm "cured," they look at two factors in the blood to determine how long I'll be on the antibiotics, and then balance that with the detrimental side effects of being on antibiotics too long. My blood work showed a dramatic improvement in both those factors, so the prognosis is only another two months. Depending on what those numbers look like then, I'll start to wean off the antibiotics . . . then more blood work to make sure the infection isn't returning as the antibiotic decreases . . . it's a long-term process. As long as those factors are even a half point above normal, I will need to stay on the antibiotics. But my doctor is very optimistic, as am I.

The strange part is that you have to be really aware of how you feel, constantly looking for potential problems and being diligent about either the infection returning or liver damage from the medication — like a slight fever, soreness around the incision or hardware, achiness, yellowness of the skin or nails, stomach aches, generally feeling unwell. It's a challenge to not overreact to symptoms or sort out "normal" pain versus a problem. (My doctor got concerned about a little splinter under my nail — which can be an indication of a heart infection. I assured him it was just a splinter.)

I try to approach it as a body scan from a mindfulness approach, as opposed to a critical, hypersensitive review of every inch of my body. It takes away the emotion and judgment, leaving me with an acceptance of whatever is ailing me instead of being worried about every little twinge. This approach has helped me to handle the pain, as well.

I am still dealing with side effects from the antibiotics, mostly hypersensitivity to the sun. So I don't get to sit by the pool much, since it's been so warm. I know you are all feeling so sorry for me right now! Let me go find my violin . . .

A big hunk of my time is spent either at physical therapy or doing my home program. PT is still very intense and usually goes at least 90 minutes. I walk out dripping wet, but I always feel better. The workout has progressed quickly and I feel really good about how far I've come. I think it's coming along faster because I was so ready for it, open to whatever I had to do, surrendering to the process and trying not to be afraid of my body and the pain. It looks like I'll only be in PT for another six weeks — which is three months less than the last time I went through this! Of course, it won't stop there and I will have to continue on my own. I am fully aware that this is, and has been, a lifetime issue and the only way to delay another round of surgery will be to stay as strong as possible.

Unfortunately, there is a real possibility that it is a case of delay versus prevent, so it changes the motivation behind it since I know I will never actually be "better." I am also fully aware that this hardware, like before, may eventually break down and have to be repaired — again. But it's a waiting game. The longer it can be put off, the more likely the techniques and hardware will be improved — just like this surgery compared to the last one. So I am completely motivated to stay out of the operating room as long as possible — especially in light of the complications that occurred this time! I prefer to sleep without the aid of anesthesia and in my own bed.

I find myself in the middle of the biggest transformation I could ever have anticipated, and the medical part seems like just a small portion of it, even though it's taking up the biggest part of my attention and time right now. But somehow, and in some way, I would have been here anyway. Life just has a way of making you face your shxx at some point.

Before I started PT, much of my process had been contemplative versus physical. PT has forced me to become more physical, which, while easy for me, has left me almost avoiding the other part. Obviously, I still have to work on integration and live less polarized. I am truly a Gemini.

I still struggle with not knowing where I'll be in three months or what my life will look like. But I suppose that's no different than most of us. I just know that I have to figure out how to live a more fully integrated life. What's tough is that, since each day is so much same old-same old and time really is abundant, there is a sense that there is always tomorrow. Sometimes I berate myself for not having it all figured out or spending more time working on it. But mostly, I remind myself to stay with surrendering. I think this lethargy or lack of pushing forward may just be part of the process, giving myself the time to heal.

As Scarlett in *Gone with the Wind* said, "I can't think about that right now. I'll think about it tomorrow." I'm sure tomorrow will come. But I'm okay if it's not today, or even the next tomorrow. I've learned that you can't push the process — either physically or spiritually. You don't really "work" at it. It just happens once you're open to it. Even exercise becomes easier if you don't "work" so hard; and you gain the greatest insights not when you're thinking, but when you relax and open to inner wisdom. How many times have we all solved a problem in our sleep?!

So maybe I'm being a little bit "Scarlett." But it's a struggle because my old beliefs would tell me that that makes me lazy. So each day, I start with reciting the Reiki Ideals (living for today, in the present moment) and an intention/affirmation/prayer (whatever you want to call it) of my own. Let me share them with you.

The Reiki Ideals
Just for today, I will let go of anger.
Just for today, I will let go of worry.
Just for today, I will give thanks for my many blessings.
Just for today, I will do my work honestly.
Just for today, I will be kind to my neighbor and every
    living thing.

And my own intention:

Today, I am thankful for the opportunity that has been given me and the support of my friends and family. I surrender to their love and this process of transformation.

Thanks, all, for listening.

June

I was climbing out of the hole a little, starting the expansion part of the process again, reaching out. I felt as though I was expanding out of my "situation," too, beginning to feel my presence in connection to the rest of the world. Even though I had never felt alone before, I realized I had made myself the center, with everyone circling around me. It was now time to join their circle. I began to feel like everyone else, and could see how everyone else was also like me. We all shared life together, and I was eager to play my part. I had taken a deep breath and began to find my voice again.

The Reiki Ideals are just what I needed to read. I am out of balance, too. Love, Carolyn

I always look forward to your emails. You're quite a courageous "Scarlett." Your strength and words help me to continue on with my own challenges. Sometimes,

I feel like giving up, but hearing from you gets me out of that rut. Donna

I am very moved by the process you are sharing. I think we all struggle in life at some level. Your words are inspiring for me. Ann

Amazing how much forward motion is hidden in the stillness. Keep doing what you're doing, and while you're doing it — try to have some fun!!! XO, Carrie

Miss Scarlett, that was beautiful. I love the Reiki Ideals. I was talking to my class the other day about surrendering . . . as in simply offering up to the universe the fact that we cannot do this alone. Help usually arrives, one way or another, usually in the form of a friend. Often a friend bearing chocolate!!! Gwen

As always, it was so wonderful to share your thoughts and feelings . . . I share my continued prayers and angels with you. Love, Liz B

I continue to pray for you and love hearing from you. You have much to offer with your insight and perspective and amazing strength. Love and blessings, Laurie

How beautiful, June. Thanks for sharing your next chapter. You are developing a tremendous amount of insight. Facing yourself in the mirror in your particular situation is ever changing. Each time you look, there appears to be a different reflection to get to know. Keep going — stay in that body — integrate right and left — and live in the gratitude that you express with every email (just beautiful). You rock, girl! Dory

Wednesday, September 1, 2010

8:38 a.m.

Re: Stuck in the middle — with me!

Hello, all!

The last couple of weeks have been somewhat eventful — unfortunately, not all good, and while I think it's been productive overall, it's another case of stepping backward to move ahead again. It became clear to me that, in order to let this new path or direction present itself, I needed to let go of some things and, in many ways, start over and, hopefully, get unstuck.

First of all, I got the rest of my blood work back and my liver function tests are significantly worse. Not to panic, though, the numbers are above normal, but not dramatically high yet. I'm not jaundiced nor do I show any real symptoms of liver damage. It warrants monitoring only because of how much the numbers have increased in just five weeks. No change in my treatment right now, except to redo the blood tests more often than planned.

Right now, I'm scheduled to go off the antibiotics in November. But if the numbers continue to go up significantly, my doctor will take me off the antibiotics early and continue periodic retesting, both for liver function and infection markers. It may be a case of letting my liver rebound and then trying another round of antibiotics afterward. Again, it's not something major to worry about at this point, but obviously a setback and something on my mind. Yellow has never been a good color for me! I was really looking forward to putting this part of my recovery behind me — still am — although it has begun to feel like I'm stuck while the rest of the world keeps moving along. Like the Stealers Wheel song (a more popular version was performed by The Steve Miller Band) — I'm stuck in the middle — but it's only with me.

I'm getting stronger in physical therapy, but it's also becoming clear that I am pretty much where I am going to be physically. It's unfortunately a case of the benefits of working harder being offset by the potential damage and increased pain levels, much like the benefits of the antibiotics being offset by their detrimental effects to my liver. From this point on, it will be maintenance mode. It also means my pain level is where I can expect it to be going forward, with the exception that I may still see some improvement neurologically. Some days are better than others, but the pain is there every day. And though I knew I wouldn't be pain free, it's a whole different matter, finally facing what I'm left with — and this daily reminder that will never go away. I'm stuck right where I am.

And so, in the interest of letting go, getting unstuck and moving forward, I made a difficult decision last week: I filed the paperwork to officially dissolve my business, Meridian Health & Fitness, and will be taking down my website soon. (Did you know you actually have to pay fees to the state to go out of business? Welcome to small business in Connecticut! Another soap box, another time.)

It was really hard to let go, as I put a lot of effort, heart and soul into creating and building the business. But I felt like it represented a life and a practice that was no longer valid or authentic for me, and it wouldn't be the right representation for whatever comes ahead. I had to let go in order to make room for something else.

In support of that decision, I began to look at where I was holding on in other ways. I felt this need to purge, to clear out the old and make room for the new — and where better to start than my closet!

In my previous life before training, I worked in the corporate world for about 25 years. Over that time, I had accumulated more than 50 suits, not to mention skirts, jackets, dresses and slacks. I had been winnowing this down over the years, but at last count I still had almost half of that in my closet. Now, why on earth would I still need 20 suits?!!!

I am ashamed to admit I also counted more than 40 sweaters, 30 fleeces and more than 50 sweatshirts! Granted, some of this dates back decades, but seriously, it was time to purge. Okay, long past time, considerably overdue . . .

And so last week, I ruthlessly attacked my closet, going through every item one by one. I now have a pile of more than 100 pieces ready to go to Goodwill — which still leaves me with way too much. I have not been stripped bare by any means!

In spite of all the new space, I don't intend to fill it with new clothes. But it was a satisfying metaphorical way to let go and make room for new. I can actually see light in my closet and maybe that will bring light to a new direction as well! It's a beautiful thing!

I continue to look at other areas in my life where I am holding on out of habit, comfort or security — material things, but also old patterns, feelings, beliefs, relationships that are keeping me from moving forward. I never realized how much of a "collector" I can be! (I can just hear some of you saying, "It's about time!")

Some of it will not be as hard as letting go of my business; and some of it will be tougher than letting go of the clothes. This purging thing is rewarding but sometimes uncomfortable, and I'm pretty certain it's an ongoing and evolutionary process. But I'm at the point in this recovery and transformation where I need to travel lighter in order to get unstuck and move ahead. The closet, the weather and the path is clear. Time to let go of the edge of the cliff.

Thanks for being my parachute!

June

After this email, I discovered I was not alone in my "stuck-ness." I'm guessing we all feel stuck at some point, with the daily grind, the obligations and responsibilities, the pains, worries and burdens. Progress, movement forward, transition — it all stalls and plateaus at some point and it requires an internal shift of perspective, a clearing out of old patterns in order to take the next step. Letting go on any level is difficult, particularly when there isn't anything new to fill it yet. Terribly scary. Tremendously vulnerable. But it's not so bad when we're all stuck in the middle together!

> *I, too, have many, many, many times been stuck. I know that doesn't feel good, but apparently, it is a common feeling for a lot of people. Sometimes it helps to know other people have the same feelings. Thanks. Donna*

> *I am grateful to be stuck in the middle with you!!! Here I am . . . stuck in the middle with you . . . and now I've got that tune stuck in my head!!! Gwen*

Tuesday, September 14, 2010

9:15 a.m.

Re: Doing well, and finally learning balance!

Hello, all!

Years ago, when I was in therapy for my knee, I went into a session with my therapist, Brian, and proudly reported that I had leg-pressed 400 pounds. And not just once — three sets of 12, on several occasions. He looked at me like I'd grown another head, and just said, "Why?"

For me, it was simple. It was a natural progression. I'd done 380 pounds; next was 400. Come on, it was a milestone! (Besides, I was working out with a friend and we bet the big burly guys next to us that I could do it . . . one of them couldn't.)

Brian pushes me hard, but at the same time he will tell you his main job is keeping me from myself — because my normal approach would be to push even harder. He constantly tells me more is not always better. But what's made it tough is I've discovered I really don't know where my end point is. With a little bit of rest, I've not yet found it. After so many years of being in pain, moving through it, functioning in spite of it, I just don't know what total fatigue feels like — or, at least, I don't let it register in my brain. Because no matter what it feels like, I just keep going. There's no other option. If I stop, I'm done — or maybe that's what I'm really afraid of.

Last week, though, at the end of the session, I said to him, "It's just possible I may be getting too old for this." He said to me, "No way. You just need to learn balance." You get inspiring lessons from the most surprising places.

I read an article about healing and made a note of this quote from Dr. David Servan-Schreiber, author of *Anticancer: A New Way of Life.* He said, "Healing is less about battling illness and more about nourishing life."

His belief, and what I've learned, is that to survive pain, illness, disability, it's more important to nurture ourselves (diet, meditation, lifestyle changes), to support the positive qualities of life which will create natural healing environments in our bodies. This new way of thinking about healing (which is actually one of the oldest ways to think about it) focuses on nurturing what's good instead of destroying what's bad — a gentle touch and a hug, instead of a sword. Life, and everything it throws at you, isn't a battle to be won or something to conquer or overcome.

And so, I have no intention of leg-pressing 400 pounds. (Okay, I may just do it once, just to see if I still can . . . I wouldn't want anyone to think I'm completely out of character!)

I am, though, really proud of how far I've come in therapy. I am way ahead of schedule from both strength and endurance standpoints, and will probably be in therapy only another couple of weeks. I've become the "poster child" for fusion surgery. I am doing well, progressing nicely. My X-rays look great and I'm building good bone, particularly in the place where it was broken down before the surgery. And I can happily report my blood work is also good — liver function and infection markers are both normal.

But at the same time, I don't feel the pressure to perform in therapy, to do more and more, or to hold up a perfect image and never admit to pain or struggle. When I say I hurt, we modify or stop. With Brian's help, I am learning balance.

That's not an excuse to slack off, though, to baby myself or not work to my potential. It just means I'm learning to listen to my body more; it's more of a mindful or mind/body approach to exercise. I put my "all" into each exercise, doing it fully, with focus on the activity itself AND the way my body feels throughout it. Not only am I getting results, but it feels good, too. I can feel compassion for the times when it's tough — and also celebrate my accomplishments.

One of the things I've struggled with over the years is integration — I could work hard physically, and work hard spiritually, but never found a way to work at both or combine them somehow. I've always felt polarized and had an all-or-nothing temperament. I'm beginning to think the physical work this time around will actually teach me to find balance and integration. Because if I can learn to find that balance physically, to integrate a mind/body approach into the physical activity . . . maybe, just maybe, it will spill over into the rest of my life.

Who knows? I may just have something here!

Thanks for listening!

With love and blessings,

June

—— ·—— ——·

This was the beginning of learning to integrate balance in my life. I don't think I knew then, though, what that really meant. But it was definitely a first step. I was cutting myself some slack, so to speak, beginning to feel that I didn't have to work so hard. In fact, when I relaxed and stopped pushing so much, I actually got more results. My "image" to others was changing — and I was okay with it.

Glad you are learning that you don't always have to be Wonder Woman! Time to practice what you preach! Sue

Balance, balance, balance. Why is it so hard for us? Gwen

Monday, October 11, 2010

My emails out began to get fewer and farther between. That didn't mean I was less connected; it meant I was assimilating, integrating, sorting. There was much information to take in and I felt like I was trying it on for size, deciding what fit, what needed adjusting and what could be discarded. But instead of "working" on it, I was attempting to simply stay open to this information, being aware of what was going on and how I felt within my body in response. The body is the best barometer we have. When we hear something, we respond to it in our bodies, one way or another. I kept listening to my body, and I was learning a lot, albeit much more slowly than I expected. I was still struggling with letting go of my old image as "strong like bull" and accepting this new reality. I was trying to find the dimmer switch when I'd spent my life either on or off. I had to find my new "truth."

10:16 a.m.

Re: Struggling for balance when reality bites!

Hello, all!

It's been a while since I've written, but I think of you daily as I struggle through this sometimes painful work — both physically and emotionally. Knowing you are all there for me, sending me warmth and caring, listening to me and completing the circle by letting me know your thoughts . . . I can't tell you how much that means to me. It has converted this difficult healing process into a wonderful journey, allowing me to open to this opportunity to grow because I am safely supported through your connection. Never in my life have I felt such loving support, I am still awed by its immensity — and humbled to be the recipient.

And so, my story continues . . .

The week before last, I "graduated" from physical therapy; and so last week I began doing the work on my own. As many of you know, it's a lot more fun, motivating and easier having someone else tell you what to do! Even for me!

My therapist had me put together a "home" program with what I thought I could handle and he reviewed it with me. I proudly put together a five-day/week program, demanding in both strength and endurance. But I'm quickly learning (it only took a week this time) I was being a little too aggressive and intense. As usual, I was trying to do too much, push too hard. Quickly, I noticed the program had my usual stamp on it — and precious little balance. How quickly we slide backward . . . what a V8 moment.

And so, when I discussed it with Brian — guess what! He was not surprised. He just let me figure it out on my own. He knew if he tried to tell me it was too aggressive, I would insist I could do it. He's a pretty smart guy, and apparently, he knows me well.

I've revised the program to be much gentler on myself, giving myself more rest time — and a lot more compassion. But the reality has definitely sunk in that I cannot do what I used to do. I cannot keep functioning in the same way — pushing through obstacles, trying to muscle through problems. Intellectually, I know this isn't the way to go, but I keep doing it. Even when you think you've already learned a lesson, somehow it always comes back to make you realize you're still in kindergarten. (But at least in kindergarten, we can still take naps!)

I remember something my dad used to tell me. He said to think of a problem as a brick wall, and there are many ways to get to the other side. He said you can dig under the wall or go over the top. He also said to remember no wall goes on forever; you can always find the ends and go around it. Unless it's a fortress — in which case, are you sure you want to get in? Fortresses hold things in as well as keep things out. Maybe the solution is in walking alongside the wall. You don't have to conquer every brick wall.

He told me that if you try to push or bulldoze through the wall, all that happens is you get bloody. I'm really tired of getting bloody. It's no wonder he used to call me Don Quixote. I've fought my share of windmills.

I am very aware that how I approach my recovery this time and what I learn will be almost a blueprint for the rest of my life. I am struggling to learn balance and compassion in my rehab and to extend that outward. I'm trying to walk alongside the wall, working with my condition and my pain, instead of pushing through it. I also think that even though I have acknowledged my condition, the need to give up my job as a trainer, and the fact this is not going away, I don't think I've fully accepted it yet as my new reality. Reality really does bite — hard! Sometimes the truth really hurts. I am still hanging on to the past image and expression of me, and I still turn to my natural desire to overcome any obstacle. Maybe that's because I haven't replaced my expression with something else yet. Maybe it's just that old habits, patterns and beliefs really and truly die hard. Maybe I really am that dense!

And so I feel a little stuck — knowing what needs to happen, but having difficulty actually integrating it . . . probably because I don't really like the reality and haven't yet let go of that emotion. I believe this is the hard part for all of us. As a dear friend and teacher of mine once said, "Enlightenment is easy; maintaining it in daily life is hard." It's easy to recognize the truth; it's a whole different story to take it in and fully believe it. Especially when that truth is hard to swallow or isn't what you thought it would be — or is challenged by everyday demands and expectations.

And so here I restate my truth . . . both the ugly and the good:

My truth is that my body will always have some difficulty doing many things, and some things are just not possible anymore. And yes, sometimes I want to scream that the truth really sucks. (Sorry, not my favorite expression, but I couldn't find a better word.) But it is also my truth that I have much to offer; and, at the right time, I will find the right package for that offering. My body is only the vehicle for my self. It is a critical part of who I am, but it does not represent everything that I am. And although my body is flawed, it does not mean I am flawed.

My truth is that it is for my highest good that I learn to integrate a kindler, gentler way of being — both physically and emotionally. It is also my truth that this is very hard to do as it requires that acknowledging it does not make me less strong in the world. I know I will take two steps forward and inevitably slide back again to old ways of thinking, old ways of being. It's just being human.

And so, with all of you as witnesses to my journey, I renew my pledge to continue integrating balance, compassion and loving kindness into my life, and to start with myself.

I will give myself the restful sleep I need to heal and not feel guilty about not being productive or what time everyone else has to get up. (I might even manage a bit of glee as I turn over in bed, snuggling deeper into the blankets, thinking of how many of you are struggling with traffic and stressful work!)

I will not feel bad if I skip a workout to enjoy lunch with a friend. And I will not always have a salad. I will take time for simple contemplation, leaving aside my list of to-dos for another day. And if I get to the end of the day and have accomplished nothing, I will revel in the pure luxury, serenity and freedom of it, and let my husband dominate dinner conversation. I will congratulate myself for understanding that doing this extends love and kindness to myself and others.

I will acknowledge I am exactly where I need to be, and I am doing exactly what I need to do right now . . . without pressure to complete the process or be anything else. I will give myself the right to simply be. I will accept that it is in my nature to want to be the best I can be, and accept the reality of what that looks like — certain that by its own definition, my best cannot be any better than it actually is. It is my truth.

And knowing all this, what I'm learning these days is that I still have so much to learn. That, too, is my truth.

With blessings and eternal thanks,

June

Stating these truths was vitally important for me. I could state my reality now in a way that seemed positive, acknowledging the difficult parts while focusing on what was good. I took myself off the hook and surrendered a little more — and it didn't feel like giving up; it felt freeing! It felt good in my body.

It sounds like you have figured out a good way to introduce a little moderation. I am proud of you. Brian (this from my physical therapist — the "sadistic" one who kicks my butt and keeps me humble — and knows me much too well!)

Yes, SKIP the salad occasionally. You only get one pass on earth and no one will know if you are "short" one lunch salad versus "up" one spicy curry! Be well . . . metta . . . Nikki

Keep on keeping on! My thoughts and prayers are with you! Carmen S

So love your insight and can totally relate. It is all about where your focus is and finding joy in the journey. I can see you smiling through the pain. You are a great example, and I know God put you in my life for more reasons. Love, Laurie

Wishing you strength and patience. XO, Cheryl

Monday, November 8, 2010

With each email I sent out, I began to think it would be my last one. I kept thinking my story had worked through its course. I worried my audience must be tired of hearing it and I doubted the value of my epistles in their lives. But encouragement kept coming, and so I continued to share what was happening physically and the thoughts and feelings those events provoked.

———~———

10:53 a.m.

Re: Good News, Bad News and Finding
the Space Between

Hello, all!
I'm beginning to notice these days that good news always seems to come with a caveat . . . good/bad, yin/yang, black/white, dark/light, joy/sorrow. I guess it's true you cannot experience one without the other — and that, I suppose, is called balance. It's also called life. And as I said before,

life is not about whether or not bad things happen to you; it's about how you respond to them.

I got the results of my blood work last week, and it was yet again a good news/bad news scenario. The good news is that my SED rate, which is the infection marker, was within normal ranges. The bad news is it's at the high end of the normal ranges and up a little from last time. The doctor says this could just be my new "normal." (After all, what is normal for me these days anyway?) The other bad news is my liver enzymes were up again, which means there's temporary damage to my liver from the antibiotics (and hopefully *only* temporary). The good news to that, though, is: To prevent further damage and give my liver the chance to recover, the doctor took me off the antibiotics!!! And the moral to this little story? Even when you have good and bad news together, you can still end on good!!! Yay!!!

I am so happy to be off the antibiotics. Not only did they make me sick most mornings, but it's a marker in time, an end to a part of this ordeal, a piece of this I can put behind me, at least for now.

The unfortunate side of this is that this infection will always be with me; it will never go away and I am left with a constant diligence about my health. If I get the flu, I have to be careful that it's not the infection returning. If I get a fever, I cannot just take a Tylenol and rest. It could be the infection. If I get soreness or tenderness in my back, it may not be a bruise or tension. It feels strange to know this thing is lying dormant within me, waiting to rise up again. And so, if I needed a lifetime, constant reminder of this process, I guess I got one.

And this is the stuff of which hypochondriacs are born! But yes, I do recognize it is also a lesson in balance, being aware enough to recognize a potential problem without dwelling on the constant threat or overreacting to every symptom — as I mentioned before, using a mindful approach, not a hypercritical awareness of my body. Not fun. But at least I'm off the antibiotics!!!

If you can't tell I'm trying desperately to focus on the positive, let me try harder. Yay!!! I've reached a milestone in my recovery! I'm off the antibiotics!

I'm trying so hard to celebrate the positive because other parts of this process keep dragging me the other way. Since I have been going through the process of filing for disability (another part of my reality I struggle with), I have been forced to face the negative side of my situation. As I sit here typing this, on my desk before me is yet another reminder of my "reality" — a handicap parking permit, a permanent one — something I never thought I'd have, no matter how handy it might be at Christmastime at the mall. And when I fill out the seemingly never-ending 10-page forms that ask me over and over again to describe everything I can't do, how much I hurt and how dreadfully useless I am, it is so hard every day to stand up and remember the opposite is true as well — that there is a lot of good going on in this process. But this negative stuff just keeps coming at me. It's forcing me to keep looking at my reality, and while that's something I just don't want to do, I know it's necessary. Yes, there is still a great part of me that doesn't want to accept my limitations, and so I keep doing things that land me in pain. I never thought I'd be here, and I keep trying to prove it wrong.

But I don't think I have blinders on. I push myself to work beyond my limits, and some of you may think I'm being stupid. But I think I'm just trying to find the boundaries. Here again, I'm looking for balance. I run at a wall, bounce off and say, "I'm not going to do that again." At least I've learned not to do it a second time! Okay, my method may not be perfect, but it seems to be working for me!

I am accepting my new limitations, but I'm trying hard not to become a victim to them or get boxed in by them. And through the disability application process, I'm realizing how hard that is. The system tries to make you a victim. And in many ways, you have to be a victim in order to meet the requirements and receive benefits. I can see how easy it is to succumb to feeling that way when everyone keeps telling you that's the truth.

And so, I continue to struggle with that contradiction, that positive/negative pull, that polar way of being. Somewhere, there is a center.

In a previous email, I talked about the struggle to find the balance between surrendering to a process while at the same time trying to grow, learn and move forward. I've found it hard to live in that middle. Some days I feel like a lazy slug; other days I have to remind myself to pull back. Some days I feel peaceful and other days I find myself getting angry with every idiot on the highway. But in the end, I must be finding the balance, because it seems easier these days to be aware of my extremes, take a breath and return to center. Bounce off a wall, learn from it and come back to center. I always thought I would have to stop living a polarized life to find integration and center. Now I know it is in that very polarization and contradiction the center exists.

I am learning to fight without fighting, to accept without accepting, to know my reality while constantly questioning it, to surrender fully without conceding responsibility and control.

I've found good has bad and bad has good; and both are the same and the opposite all at the same time. And somewhere in the middle is the truth. A life of contradictions brings peace; there is no balance without extremes, no constancy without change, no center without everything spinning around it. And this is where I exist.

Now if I could just keep myself from bouncing off walls to get there!

With love and thanks for your continued support,

June

This was quite a revelation for me, this idea that balance exists in extremes. It was the first time I really believed I was growing and learning. I had thought I needed to find an even-keel way to live, but that's just complacency and doesn't encompass the passion I knew I needed. Buddha says there is no joy without pain, no peace without unrest. Balance is not about never experiencing extremes; it's about being aware of where you are and gently coming back to center, coming back to the breath and the source.

I envisioned a child's toy top, spinning madly — yet amid the spinning madness, the center of the top was still. Absolutely still.

So love how you HONESTLY express and share your heart. Can so identify with you. It is so easy to buy into "victim" mentality, but there's no life there. Know I love and treasure you — beautiful inside and out. Love, Laurie

I've been told you are never truly in balance. There will always be something that pulls you off center, so it's a constant re-balancing. I use the Five Pillars of Health for my balance check — Healthy Mind, Body, Family, Society and Finances. I just see how I can keep each ball off the ground every day. Thank you for continuing to share your journey. It has helped me keep my need to balance in the front of my mind. Love, Carolyn

Monday, December 20, 2010

The holidays were approaching and I hadn't sent out an email in more than a month. I was missing that connection, but still afraid to "bother" my friends further. But I found I had more to say — there was someone I wanted to talk about — and they were still eager to listen.

12:42 p.m.

Re: Happy Holidays, best-laid plans — and then what really happens!

Hello, all!
It's been a while since I've written to all of you, so I thought I'd take advantage of the holidays to send out an email to wish you all health and happiness, and send you much love and gratitude!

There is nothing new to report, except the winter weather has been challenging to my pain levels and mobility. I am due to have more blood work in a few weeks to check on liver enzymes; I also have an appointment with my spine doctor coming up in January. So right now, it is just status quo. I'm a little worried, because I have been experiencing some stabbing pain mid-back and increased numbness and tingling in my right leg. But I continue to remain hopeful that all is well. And overall, I feel okay.

As the end of the year approaches, it has been interesting to look back. I am amazed that much of this past year's experience now seems like a dream. Sometimes it's hard to believe it actually happened. I have tried not to relive the past 10 months by dwelling on it; I prefer to keep looking forward. But some retrospection is always helpful to learn from all that's happened and check in on where I am now.

A year ago, I had no way to predict all of this. No frame of reference to conceive this would be possible in any way. I never expected everything wouldn't always go as I planned it. Obviously, I was not short on ego.

I didn't expect my body would break down and fail me. I didn't know I would be left with no means of supporting myself, completely dependent for the first time in my life. I didn't have any idea. Life is what happens when your best-laid plans don't happen.

No, this year has not gone as planned, and I'm sure you all will think I'm crazy when I tell you I believe that it is a good thing. I have experienced great pain and disappointment, yes. But I've also experienced incredible love, friendship, support and the beauty of simple caring. I have been shown real goodness, kindness and gentleness of spirit. And though I will never completely lose the Type-A part of me, I believe this experience has changed me. It has allowed me to surrender in a way I could never have learned otherwise — which tells you a little about how bullheaded I can be.

It has been a year of absolute acceptance — acceptance of what is real, right now, without being concerned about what has happened previously and what will happen tomorrow. This was easy to do when I was really sick with the infection after the surgeries. When you're that sick, you really can't be anywhere except where you already are. There is no energy for anything other than the present moment. It gets harder when you feel okay, but it's still a good lesson to have learned, even if I did have to learn it the hard way.

But give me a moment and let me tell you something about my husband, Peter. He is not what I would call a religious or spiritual person. His view on life is pretty simple: He believes in enjoying it. When he was in high school, he was assigned to write a paper on the "purpose of life." The premise for his paper was that the entire purpose of life was to have sex — after all, the most essential function of life is to recreate life, to procreate, and the only way for humans to do that was to have sex. He got an F on the paper; but, after an appeal, the teacher reluctantly gave him an A. Even now, his theory says something about how he lives his life.

To Peter, life is simple, and this is what's important to him:

- No matter what you do for a job, work hard and do it to the best of your ability.

- Do whatever you have to do to take care of your family.

- Be loyal and generous to your friends.

- Never pass by an opportunity to be a Good Samaritan.

- Play outside whenever possible.

- Drink beer and eat ice cream (the good stuff, not the low-fat).

Well, except for the beer and ice cream, I think he has something. He doesn't worry about what's around the corner, he just enjoys every day the best way he can, open to opportunities to be of service to himself and others. He experiences life with passion and, of course, that comes with some pain. But he accepts the entire package and lives each moment with a fullness that is enviable.

And so, as the end of the year approaches, I choose not to dwell on what has already happened. It's done and holds no reality for me anymore. I choose not to worry about or try to force what will happen tomorrow. That too does not exist and will only be real when it becomes today's experience — and I choose not to waste today with something that is not even real. All those gurus and yogis have been right all along: There is really only this moment.

Last year for Christmas, we received a gift of a very expensive bottle of champagne. It has been in our fridge for an entire year. I kept looking for and waiting for the right time to open it. And yet our anniversary and birthdays passed, along with many physical milestones. Was nothing worthy of celebrating with this champagne? Was I still looking around the corner for something better?

And so yesterday, I got up and saw it was going to be a nice day — some cloudiness, but mostly blue skies. And I realized it was just like my life — some challenges, but mostly so very much to be happy about. It was more than enough reason to celebrate.

And so we opened that bottle of champagne.

Cheers, everyone!

June

I had really turned a corner and was settling into my new body (or as Dory had pointed out, the same body I'd had all along). I was settling into my new life, with its activities and purpose. But most of all, I was filled with an incredible gratitude for everyone in my life who was so special to me — my husband, my friends, my son, my doctor and my physical therapist. I felt nurtured and cared for, and loved beyond imagination, simply for being me. It amazed and humbled me.

Once again, I received an email from a friend with a story to share. Just as I was, yet again, considering stopping the emails, she let me know my words meant something and had arrived at precisely the right time for her. I am still in awe of this process and how the act of merely reaching out somehow is so healing — to both parties. I truly believe the very act of sharing our stories somehow lessens the burdens of each of us. I had never felt so connected in my life.

Your email spoke to me and helped me in so many ways. You reminded me of two very important things — acceptance and staying present. Thank you for this Christmas gift. ☺ And please keep sending these emails as you never know who will need it!!! Thank you again for sharing. Allie

Your emails have been inspirational and awesome throughout the year. The Finnish people have a word, "sisu". It means courage, tenacity, dedication, determination, resolve, an unwillingness to cave in to whatever the problem is. I would apply all of this to you, plus faith. Eileen F

Cheers to you, too! Merry, merry Christmas — and here's to a healthy, pain-free 2011. XOXO Sue

It is so wonderful that your husband has been completely supportive of you. I love his outlook — even the ice cream part. Thank you so much for sharing your journey and insights with me. I, too, am blessed with many caring friends and mentors. Know that I hold you in my heart, and that I love and respect you so much. Lots of love, Leslie

I enjoy your words . . . some sad . . . some make me laugh. But mostly the inspiration and courage you have. Your works excite and inspire me. Love, Ann

Thank you for sharing Peter's list. He is on to something. I love you, my dear friend. Carolyn

Your spiritual practices are amazing and inspiring! I'm so happy to hear you are celebrating yourself and your marriage and your life — even when it's not what you imagined. That is certainly the challenge. I wish you every possible blessing. Peace and love, Cheryl

So happy to hear that you celebrated with the champagne! Lovely . . . so perfect . . . so true . . . the message is so clear and simple. Thank you!!! I hope the new year brings you much joy. Debbie

Friday, February 11, 2011

11:49 a.m.

Re: Bug Free and Living a Gerbil's Life

Hello, all!

Well, one chapter of this challenging year has finally come to a close. I had my blood work done again this week and all markers (liver, kidneys, infection and inflammation) are back to normal, which means the staph infection (and resulting organ impact) is now under control! There will always be the possibility it will return — it never truly goes away — and I will have to premedicate with antibiotics for dental work and (God forbid) future surgeries, but I am really relieved there is no permanent damage. Right now, I am bug free!!! (Or at least bug sleeping peacefully.)

Even though I've had to deal with these health issues, some people have remarked that I have an easy life right now, a dog's life. And in some ways, it's like that. Yes, I don't have much responsibility, and I get housed and fed and clothed and loved. (I refuse to be scratched behind the ears!) I don't work much and I'm able to spend a lot of time just doing things for me — reading, meditating, listening to music, writing, working out. You might even say I'm getting a little bit spoiled — there's that princess thing in me again! (No, I don't watch the soaps — but I do watch Law & Order reruns.) But it's not a dog's life. We're not meant to live that way, or at least I'm not. It's more like a gerbil's life.

Lately, I've felt a little like a gerbil on a wheel, just spinning round and round, waiting for things to change, waiting for something to happen, waiting for this slow healing. I know it's just where I am right now, and I am so grateful for the space and security I have to be able to do this. And I know the wheel is going to stop eventually and I'll be able to move forward, but it's been frustrating — I don't do this patience thing very well, in case you didn't know. Especially when I can't do anything about it. And I find myself a little distracted and restless because of it. I tell myself to focus and not struggle or push too hard. Surrender, without losing control. Having the staph infection off my list makes me hope the wheel is starting to slow down. It's one more thing to check off so I can move forward.

What keeps me on that wheel? Well, some of it is the reality of my physical limitations and the intention to do something that will not further harm my body. In case you're wondering, I do not want more surgeries! I've learned no matter how much passion you have for something, if it harms you in some way, it's not the right path. It's so tempting sometimes to go back to training, but I keep in mind how much I've struggled with integration of mind and body — and I've learned you can't sacrifice one for the other. Passion over pain? I don't think so.

The other thing that keeps me on that wheel is the whole process of applying for Social Security Disability. I struggle with it because the system makes you feel like a victim, forcing you to concentrate on what you can't do instead of what you can do. To win, you have to lose. I've always chosen to ignore what I can't do. And I've always taken pride in being strong and capable. My well-known intense workouts, requiring both strength (will and determination) and high endurance (perseverance), leave me feeling great, both physically and emotionally — in pain, but great. But here again, I'm faced with integrating mind and body. It's ego that gives me that pride, and ego is the mind telling you what's important — yes, sometimes to the detriment of the body.

It's okay to have an ego, that's what makes us human. And I certainly don't want a life without passion. But neither should be the sole driver; and if the outcome harms me physically, it can't be right. It's that whole mind/body thing. We are not one or the other, and I'm learning to find the balance between the two.

I've been searching — intellectually, emotionally and spiritually — for what my next step is, once the healing is progressed, the disability issue is determined and I can get off that wheel. But I haven't yet found it. I have some ideas brewing, but I don't think what I'm looking for traditionally exists. I may have to create it. How do I find something that gives me passion, satisfaction, pride and a sense of connection — and nourishes my body as well? That's not much to ask for, is it?

In the meantime, I have a gerbil's life until I find the answer that allows me to build that integration. I know living in that balance and integration is a key component to my next step. The main thing, though, is I can't let this search distract me or keep me from living now, enjoying what I have today. If I never find this thing I'm looking for, I will still have all that I am blessed with right now. And I can't let myself forget the simplicity of living a life of present moments with friends, family and incredible love, peace and support. I think the real secret is just that — enjoy and gain satisfaction from whatever it is you're doing without guilt, regret or negative thinking — whether it's healing the sick (or yourself), working a deli counter, managing a corporate job, being a mom, eating chocolate — or being a gerbil.

But I think my wheel is starting to squeak!

With love,

June

The responses encouraged me to stay present, to listen to all the lessons I'd learned so far; at the same time, they acknowledged my frustration. Long ago, I realized the value of these emails for me was in their honesty. Even when I was frustrated, sad, angry or feeling negative, it would be important to express these feelings without censoring or trying to always appear perky and positive. I knew these feelings would be received with support, compassion, non-judgment and encouragement.

So happy to hear your good news! I can relate to everything you said — beautiful, true and painful all at the same time. Much wisdom and insight. Be blessed, my dear friend. Laurie

This is wonderful news that the little buggers have gone dormant! That is a huge weight lifted. Continue to take this time to be good to yourself. I think we women tend to put ourselves last and don't take the five minutes we need to care for ourselves. Be well, my friend, and thank you for sharing. Love, Carolyn

Dear June, your courage and humor are a delight. May every cell in your body find and maintain its divine right placement. Love, Cheryl

Congratulations! Thanks for keeping me up to date on this journey of yours. If I may make a comment — you'd be surprised how wonderful and relaxing a little rubbing behind the ears can make you feel. I say, dog or no dog, go for it! XO, Carrie

Monday, March 14, 2011

10:58 a.m.

Re: A Year Later

Hello, all!

It's been a year now since the first of my last round of surgeries (3/12). One year ago today, I was in a vastly different place. For one thing, I'm not on morphine and sleeping all day! Ah, the good ole' days . . . !

Back then, after those surgeries and the subsequent loss of my career, while I was dealing with the staph infection, my husband said he thought it was going to be a year of transformation for me. I thought that was pretty intuitive, since that hadn't even occurred to me yet. (Blame it on the morphine. The brain wasn't really working well then.) He was right, of course. But I don't think I have the same idea of what that means now as I did a year ago. A transformation. Reinventing myself. Change. New and improved. That's what I thought would happen. I was excited!

And yet, I don't really feel much different today.

Physically, I am different, of course. I have good days and bad days, but that's better than having all bad days. I hurt, and sometimes I handle that pain better than other times. In fact, my husband said to me this morning, "It might just be possible you're not as young as you used to be, you know." Now, wasn't that sweet of him?!!! But he's right. My body is a lot less forgiving, and I feel it.

Emotionally, there are subtle differences. I think my relationships are better. I try to handle situations with more compassion and understanding; I've certainly learned a lot about myself. And I've learned how to surrender, find balance, relax and stay open to possibilities.

But I expected the year to bring me a new "set of clothes," a new outward expression. Instead, what happened is I got stripped bare and started over from scratch — and it's taken the year for me to at least feel a little comfortable walking around naked.

I've realized this transformation wasn't to create a new me; it was to help me to be more of who I already am. And that's why it doesn't feel so different. I expected a metamorphosis, a major shift, a new skin, a new way of living that would integrate mind and body. What lofty goals! To do so, I thought I had to completely change who I was and how I deal with pain or handle physical or emotional discomfort. But it isn't like that. It's like coming back to where I've been all along. If you try to change yourself into something that's not you, it will never stick.

To explain how this is so, let me digress a moment to tell you some ancient history. Some of you may already know this: When I was 19, I was raped. It was what they now call "acquaintance rape." I survived the, um, "episode" by doing what I'd always been able to do well: disassociate from my body. I went to another place in my mind and got through it. It was a skill I'd learned as a child when it was important for me to escape, one that created a pattern of how I would deal with painful situations for much of my life. Escape meant survival. I couldn't be in my body. It hurt there and I would have to remember what was done to me. Disassociating served me well. The more pain I was in, the more I'd leave my body and let it go numb. You couldn't have found someone less in touch with her body if you'd tried. But I sure could handle pain.

Eventually, knowing there was another side and wanting to be more mind/body connected, I swung the pendulum in the other direction and became intensely physical. But not when it came to dealing with my physical or emotional pain. I still automatically resorted to old ways. And it continued to serve me well, even though I believed it wasn't helping me to live an integrated life. This year's journey has been part of that search for a mind/body connection.

I began to listen to my body more, and it sure had a lot to tell. I did not go through this year with flying colors. There were lots of days and nights of crying with the pain, dealing with the loss, the insecurity, the uncertainty, the futility, the physical debilitation and the emotional rawness of no longer knowing who I was or what I had to contribute. If I didn't show it, trust me, I was a wreck.

I didn't let it rule my life, and there were many, many positives throughout the year; but the struggle was there, nonetheless. And sometimes, it was difficult to see an end or a way out. If it wasn't for the support from all of you, I'm not sure I would be here to tell the story now.

As parents, we spend the first two years of our children's lives eager for them to start walking and talking — and then the next 18 years wishing they would just sit down and shut up! It was like that for me. I wanted to connect more to my body, but now I just wished my body would go away again!

I thought, though, I would have to give up that pattern of disassociating, that ability to shut off my body when I needed to. I thought I was learning a "better" way, a different way. But what happened was I didn't give up that skill, I just learned to develop another aspect of me, one that already existed, to add to it — awareness. I learned I didn't have to change me, I could just become more of who I already am. I don't feel different because I'm still me.

There are times when that disassociation is really useful, trust me, but not without awareness. I think it's okay to shut off the signals from the body, but not automatically — and not before understanding the message the body is delivering. And it's even okay recognizing when you can't handle hearing the message right now. It's absolutely fine if you have to tell your child to sit down and be quiet, but if you can, it's important to try to hear what he or she has to say first. It's like that for me now.

No matter how many battles we have to fight, how many twists and turns our lives go through, doesn't it always seem as though we come back to where we've been before? That's not the futility of life going around in circles; it's because each time we make the circle, we become more of who we already are. We can more fully express and accept ourselves — our strengths, faults and desires.

Change or transformation implies there is something in us to fix, something inherently wrong that absolutely must be extinguished or improved. But that's not true. We already have everything we need within us, and everything within us has value. To extinguish or change it would mean losing a part of ourselves. The trick is to be aware, accept and listen to ourselves — all of ourselves, even those parts we wish would just sit down and shut up! I can grow and learn without losing or changing me.

Early on in this process I posed a question to myself and knew I would have to find the answer: How can you be where you are, who you are, accept that place and find happiness and at the same time move forward and grow? When I started this, that question confused me. And I didn't realize how important that question would be. But now, I believe I'm beginning to understand. And if I'm not explaining it well enough, it's because the concept cannot be explained with just the mind. It's something that must be felt in the body as well, without words. The mind would find it to be full of contradictions, but that's okay, because a balanced and integrated life is also full of contradictions.

I look around and realize we are constantly bombarded with messages that tell us we have to change, to improve — with beauty makeovers and plastic surgery and the abundance of self-help books that hold the secret to fixing whatever it is we're not happy with. It's getting harder and harder to simply be happy in our own skin and to be comfortable expressing who we really are without feeling judged. I spent most of my life striving for the next battle, the next challenge, the next conquest, always believing the grass was greener on the other side of the fence. If I could just accomplish more, lose more weight, be more beautiful, be smarter and better than ever — then, I would be happy.

But now, I know if I can just simply be who I already am and all of who I am, I'll be happy in whatever pasture I'm in. There are lots of weeds and dandelions, and I wouldn't give them up for the world. Because I can see now that the grass is really quite green.

With much love,

June

I felt I was finally circling around to find out who I was, without a role to fall back on. And discovering it wasn't about a fix or a change, but more about becoming more fully me — well, that was a great relief. I felt more raw than ever before, but it didn't leave me feeling vulnerable. I could finally and forever drop that armor and that sword I had said I would drop a year ago. There was no fight in me anymore. But instead of feeling defeated, I felt peaceful.

Isn't it the truth that when we are stripped bare, we wonder what is there underneath? Everything is so primal, so basic, brought down to the bare essence. And I like your essence . . . or should I say, effervescence?!!! Grateful you let me be part of you this year. Love, Gwen

Amen! You really struck a chord with me with this one, my dear friend. Thank you for being so brave to share you innermost thought with us. It helps us to see things more clearly. I love you! Carolyn

How wonderful to hear your healthy voice. It has indeed been a long and difficult road for you this year, but you have emerged into a more evolved conscious plane, and a wiser one at that! I, too, bristled at my husband's comment, "I was wondering when you'd realize you're no spring chicken anymore, Liz!" But it was spoken with love and concern for my well being and allowed me to release some "shoulds" and embrace changes that turned out to be improvements to my life instead of deficits. I applaud your accomplishments this year, and celebrate you. Liz B

I can only say a big YES to all your insights, the power of awareness and the choice that can follow from awareness . . . the acceptance for what is, and at the same time, still holding an intention for transformation, but open ended and with acceptance for the outcome. Love, Doris

Well, you've succeeded in bringing me to tears. All of your messages have been important and inspiring, but none more so than this one. Thank you so much for sharing you — all of you — with us. XO, Carrie

I am reminded now of something I said at the start of this book, at the time not knowing the outcome.

Once upon a time . . . there was a girl who searched the world over for the next battle to be won, only to find herself where she had been all along.

And the Story Ends — For Now

Friday, April 15, 2011

9:24 a.m.

Hello, all!

Over the last year, I have truly enjoyed writing to all of you and I have been blessed with an abundance of loving, supportive and insightful responses. It has made a difficult year — and a challenging prognosis for the future — one that allowed me to grow and learn on so many levels.

But with this last email, I feel it's time for the story to end, at least for now. I finally did get my disability claim approved, and with that uncertainty settled and medically well on the road back to health, it felt like the story had played itself out. It's time to put a period on the end of this very long sentence.

And so I have one final chapter to tell. Buckle up, get comfy, it's almost over . . . time to roll the credits!

Often when you look around, you find metaphors in your life that represent something more than what they seem to be. If you look closely, you'll find parts of your life that are shining examples of great lessons to be learned. It can be something your child says or does, a book you selected seemingly at random, a conversation with a friend, or something you do all the time that has been sitting right in front of you, saying, "Look at me! I have the answers you've been looking for!" An epiphany from the simplest sources. The GE light bulb.

Spinning (or what is now sometimes called Indoor Cycling) suddenly became that metaphor for me.

Some of you may already know this, but I'm an avid Spinner, completely hooked. I think people either love or hate Spinning. And when you love it, sometimes people look at you like you're nuts. To me, it's like meditating on a bike. I can sink into the music, get into the rhythm and connect to my body and to the bike in a way that gives me that runner's high. There's something incredibly centering in the intense movement — much like finding the center in the middle of chaos that I spoke of a few emails ago.

Recently, I joined a new gym and began trying out new classes and instructors. With the new environment, I tried to be more aware of what was happening to me during class. I'd been Spinning for so long it had become second nature. I wanted to discover what it was that made it such a good experience for me.

What I learned was the way I approached Spinning — which I'd been doing for more than 15 years — was exactly the kind of integration, surrender and balance I'd been looking for in the rest of my life. I already had the secret, the "how"; I just didn't know it. Just like Dorothy in *The Wizard of Oz*, who already had the means to get her heart's desire — to go home — I was standing right in front of the answers I was looking for. Or more accurately, I was sitting on them.

When I'm on a bike, I'm relaxed. I surrender to the music and the rhythm of the class. I wear comfortable clothes and don't care about having the perfect gym outfit on. My hair is a mess. I am completely me. I connect my body to the bike and the music, and often to the energy of the rest of the people in the class. Even when the intensity increases, my breathing stays even. And when certain parts of my body hurt, I don't fight it. I simply acknowledge it and ask myself if it's the kind of pain that says "stop." If not, I relax into the pain and let my body find its natural motion, becoming one with the bike and letting each movement naturally flow from one to the next.

By the end of the class, my clothes are soaked, my ponytail is dripping and I know I've worked hard. But my breathing is usually not labored and I feel unbelievably peaceful. I am completely relaxed in my form, so it seems effortless.

Amazing. Something I've been doing all along has encompassed everything I've struggled to learn over the last year. It is truly amazing how life seems to come full circle — but each time you complete the circle, you know a little more and can be more fully yourself.

In the middle of this major transformation, I thought it meant I was going to dramatically change. Instead, I found it's more like getting a sea-salt body scrub that takes off the outer layer of dead skin, leaving the next layer (next one, not new one — it's been there all along) glowing and vibrant. That layer is closer to my center, my core. I feel like more of "me" can show through.

When my doctor was planning my surgery last year, he told me he wasn't going to correct the curvature that was there. He was just going to re-fuse in order to support the back as is. My spine had curved back to around 35 degrees, which isn't perfect but also isn't horrible. (Twenty is normal; it had previously been corrected to 22 degrees.) The curvature had been holding steady at 35 for a while, not curving more. The thought was this was apparently where my back wanted to be naturally. He didn't try to "fix" my back. He just gave it what it needed for support so it could be stable and strong. I didn't know how prophetic this would be, but isn't that what this last year has been all about? I got the support I needed from all of you that allowed me to simply be . . . me.

And so here it is, this is what I learned about being "me" — and, being as stubborn as I am, the lessons were not easily learned.

> *You may be "what you eat," but you aren't what you "do."*
> And when you strip away all those roles and possessions, it's truly scary to find out what's lying underneath. I had to shift my belief structure about what constituted value, and I could do that because of the constant encouragement,

support and love I received — even when I wasn't "doing" anything. When you can look at yourself this way, you can look at others that way, too; and it makes it easier to be less judgmental and find more compassion and forgiveness. We are not our actions or our work. We are simply our thoughts, our words, our feelings. If I choose to make mine compassionate and loving, I will be compassionate and loving. Buddha says, "The mind is everything. What you think, you become." And I don't know about you, but to me, that has more value than any job on this planet.

Surrender.

And when you think you've surrendered, check in on yourself. Chances are there's another level of surrender. It's like tension. We hold tension in our bodies and sometimes don't feel it because we're so used to it being there. It's the same thing with control. We're so used to being in control that even though we say we've surrendered, a little part of us is still holding on tightly to whatever control the ego says it needs to survive. But it is when we can completely let go of our daily masks, armors, swords and just for once stop fighting, pushing, driving, struggling — that's when our natural abilities and spirit take over. That's when real growth occurs. If you're still fighting your pain or your stress or your problems, you won't win. Why on earth would I want to fight a losing battle anyway? And I thought I was smart . . .

Pain is a part of life.
Trying to push it away, ignore it or fight it will only make it scream louder. By embracing the pain as a part of life, part of living a complete and full life, it can no longer control our thoughts and emotions. In fact, detaching from the emotion of pain will always diminish it. Buddha says there is no joy without sorrow, no peace without suffering. At the same time, becoming the pain, identifying with it or becoming a victim to it will only leave you constantly wallowing in it. Pain may be a part of life, but it doesn't have to become your life. I can embrace the pain, acknowledge and accept it because I know there is joy on the other side. It's not trying to tell me something is wrong. It just is.

Growth is a circle.
Change is not about what we have to fix. It's about learning how to be more of who we already are. Our journeys and our paths are not linear. We always find ourselves coming back to what we know, back to where we already are. But each time, we've learned a little more about who we

really are, and have more courage to be that way.

Balance can be passionate.
Living a balanced life doesn't have to mean everything is always even-keel. In fact, I believe it's the opposite. And much like those who try to eliminate thoughts while meditating — it's just not possible. Do you know anyone who's happy all the time? Someone who seems to handle everything calmly, never a hair out of place, never flustered, never raising their voice? Their lives are perfect? Always with a smile and a soft word? Well, one, they're lying. And two, don't you just want to smack that smile off their face?! I've discovered balance exists in extremes — being aware of those extremes, experiencing them and then coming back to center. Feeling passion, sorrow, pain, joy, exhaustion, the rush of adrenaline — it's what creates life. Balance, like Growth, is not linear. It is not a straight road. It's more like driving through the streets of Boston.

Acceptance.
When we can truly accept our reality of the moment, we can give up the fight for perfection. I'm telling you, at least for me, that ship has sailed. If I keep trying to swim after it, I'll get

really exhausted and probably drown. Real change comes from acceptance of who you are — in all your strengths and faults — and accepting what is the real you with compassion and love. When you truly accept yourself, change (or growth) happens effortlessly and naturally.

You've seen the people who are genuinely comfortable in their own skin. Don't they look beautiful, no matter what they look like physically? Finding this acceptance, though, is hard. I don't know about you, but my life has been filled with people eager to criticize me for one thing or another. Whenever I would go home to visit, I was always told my hair was either too short or too long. I was either too fat or too skinny. I was either dressed too casually or too formally. I talked too much or too little. For the love of God and country, I just could not get it right! And because of their criticism, it taught me I had to constantly change, improve or fix something about myself.

And now? There are still critics in my life. That's okay. There's always something to learn. But at each moment, I can accept who I am at that moment — imperfect, sure . . . flawed, absolutely. But that's okay, too. Because it's way too much effort to be anything other than who I am. And so I have two choices: I can accept who I am . . . or waste my life fighting it. If you remember, I gave up my sword a long time ago. I'm not picking it back up now.

Thank you, all, for listening to me over this last year and for sharing in this incredible journey. I know it's not over, but I've bent your ears and taken your attention long enough. With your permission, I may periodically send out a hello, with a story to tell, an experience or another hard lesson learned. I hope you will do the same with me.

My body is scarred, crooked and in pain. And I have never felt better in my life. I owe this to all of you. I could never have gotten here without you.

With much love and eternal gratitude,

Namaste.

June

I looked forward to receiving these final responses. I knew they would celebrate my journey and continue to provide great insight while offering me the unconditional love I'd basked in for the last year. I felt a little like a child finally learning to stand up on her own, or a ship that had finally come home after a long journey. And I could do so because I knew the arms of my friends would be there to catch me should I ever fall.

Dear June, How beautifully written. As I have read your incredible journey over this past year or so I have

213

admired your honesty and courage. Kudos to you and I wish you continued healing and growth. Fondly, Carmen S

Can't believe it has been over a year — wow. What a journey for you. Glad you are happy. Love, Sue

As always, thank you for sharing and baring it all! Your words will touch everyone in their own way. I particularly loved your wit in this installment, "swimming after the ship that has sailed." I will be home soon. We have to have a bottle on the beach! I love your crooked center to pieces! Love, Carolyn

God Bless you, June. God Bless you. Xoxoxo Carrie

I'm going to miss your updates. I hope you stay strong, mentally and physically. You have come so far, and should be proud of yourself. I think of you often and sometimes picture you pushing me like you used to when I work out. Take care, Sue M

I was very touched by your writing and the description of the insights you have gained over the last year. I can only say a big YES to all your insights — the power of awareness and the choices that can follow.... the acceptance of what is and, at the same time, still holding an intention for transformation, but an open-ended one with acceptance for the outcome. Love, Doris

Your story is a beautiful one, yet painful. Your journey is not the end, yet just the beginning . . . and you are always in my prayers. Hugs, Dee

I feel blessed to walk with you through this experience. Thank you for sharing. Ann

Wow! Well said! Well done! Your journey on many levels is our journey, too. Thank you for sharing the good, the bad and especially the wisdom. So much of what you said is simply true and reading your words I quietly kept saying YES! Our wisdom is like a treasure within but we don't always dig deep enough until there is a crisis or someone like you puts into words what we know to be true in our hearts. I wish you all the best! Kim

Your story is not ending. It's beginning. ☺ Love, Gwen

Dear June, another deep bow to you, your journey and the wisdom that flows from you. Love and blessings, Cheryl

You absolutely gorgeous thing, you! Bravo! Bravo! Bravo! So beautiful . . . Unlimited hugs to you, sweet one! Dory

And lastly, a dear friend and teacher celebrated how far and wide I'd searched to finally come home and find "me."

As I read the summary of your journey, I could not help reflecting on all we have shared over the years — this wonderful odyssey of evolution, transformation, courage and stubbornness! I am truly honored to have been a part of this unfolding. As I wrote to you many months ago, I stated that I will be there, in dreams and in the awakening. I have been there in your dreams, and now I am here again to celebrate an even greater realization of your Divine Essence! Yet again I say, your greatest expression is yet to be told!

As a ship sails through the darkness and fog, there is comfort in the Light upon the distant shore. Its job is to guide the way home, to steady the path of the weary sailor. One day, the ship returns to the shore. The Light is waiting. As the ship arrives, its own Light radiates with such intensity that it pales the sun. And the Light upon the shore is warmed by its glow. Welcome home. Namaste. Richard

Sticking My Finger
in the Light Socket of Love

With a little over a year of this unbelievable journey behind me, I found myself struggling with how to end the story. (And I thought the beginning was hard!) I realized this journey was not about trying to get somewhere else; it was about working at being where I already am and being there more fully, more present. I've also learned real healing — whether physical or emotional — requires an openness and acceptance. And, most importantly, it requires a tuning in to connectedness, welcoming and accepting the support and love of others; becoming aware of the notion that we are not alone in our healing, that there are kind, gentle hands ready, able and eager to help — and taking those hands in ours. It was like sticking my finger into a light socket and being connected to this incredible loving energy, one that held on and wouldn't let me go, no matter what I said. Seeking out this connection and accepting it was probably the greatest lesson I learned this year. It was truly a humbling lesson, one that left me in awe of the healing power of the love of others around me.

Someone recently said to me that I am fortunate to have so many people in my life to stand by me as they have done in this journey. And yes, I am deeply blessed. But I also believe we all have networks of friends, family, colleagues — even strangers — who are eager to help, if we just ask for it. We don't have to go it alone! We all have a light socket of love we can plug into.

I used to tell my son, "Don't ask, don't get." Well, the more spiritual version of that is, "Ask, and you shall receive." But we all seem to have such trouble asking for help when we need it. That, too, was difficult for me. I was so comfortable being a strong warrior who fought her battles on her own. To lay myself bare? To let everyone know I wasn't quite as strong as I let on and that I hurt and was really scared? Really tough. But in the end, yet another lesson learned: I discovered it takes a lot more courage to be vulnerable than it does to be strong. Being vulnerable in front of another human being is probably one of the hardest things we can do. And yet, it is perhaps one of the most healing. You'll be surprised. Just ask. We are all ready and willing to help.

We're taught so much to fight through life. But life is not supposed to be so hard, is it? Why is it we find it so difficult to ask others to support us with love and compassion? To relax and surrender to the moment? To be part of that moment — living *in* it, not through it or past it.

Acceptance and gratitude. Acceptance of the love that surrounds me and gratitude for the opportunity to be loved and to take this journey. Acceptance of my reality, acceptance of myself. And gratitude for all that I am — and all that I am not. That's where I find myself today. Quite unexpectedly, I found grace.

And so at this moment, I can honestly say . . . My center is crooked!

And I'm okay with it.

Thank you, from the bottom of my heart, for listening and sharing in my story. Namaste.

About the Author

As a Meditation Teacher, Reiki Master and MindBody Coach, June Hyjek offers extensive experience in pain and stress management, working with clients to help them move through life's transitions with grace and peace. Her practice emphasizes techniques that work to create physical, emotional and spiritual fitness.

June is a graduate of the Advanced Training Program at the Center for MindBody Medicine, with a focus on mindbody therapies for pain and stress. In addition to her training at the Center, she has studied and continues to practice a wide variety of meditation techniques, including mindfulness, transcendental, Chi Kung, chanting and mantras, as well as many Buddhist and Hindu practices.

June's workshops are geared to give participants real-life practical and holistic solutions for achieving and maintaining wellness. She regularly conducts workshops on pain and stress management, meditation, nutrition and mindful eating, the chakras, and transition management.

In 2009, June released her meditation CD, *Moving into Grace*. The meditation uses the imagery of gentle movement to help the listener experience freedom in the body and the release of stress and pain. The CD has allowed many clients to find a place of center, balance, peace — and Grace.

Certified by the Aerobics & Fitness Association of America, June's expertise also includes traditional fitness practices with specializations in chronic disease, spinal stabilization, orthopedic disabilities, eating disorders and senior fitness. Although recently deemed "medically retired" from an active role as a personal trainer, June continues to coach her clients on incorporating exercise, movement and nutrition in the management of pain and stress. She is also certified with Lee Hecht Harrison in Transition Management and with Body Balance University in Mat Pilates.

Personally, June has struggled with the debilitating condition of scoliosis for more than half her life. She has overcome the pain and emotional issues from six surgeries, finding healing through mindbody approaches and the loving support of others. She continues to use her personal experience and shares her insights on pain in her blog, *Transcending Pain and Stress*. (http://transcending painandstress.blogspot.com)

More information on June can be found on:

LinkedIn: http://www.linkedin.com/pub/june-hyjek/3/329/482

Facebook: http://www.facebook.com/home.php#!/profile.php?id=1654751112

For more information on scoliosis, please visit the website for the National Scoliosis Foundation: http://www.scoliosis.org.